# Contents

# List of Designers

DD 5

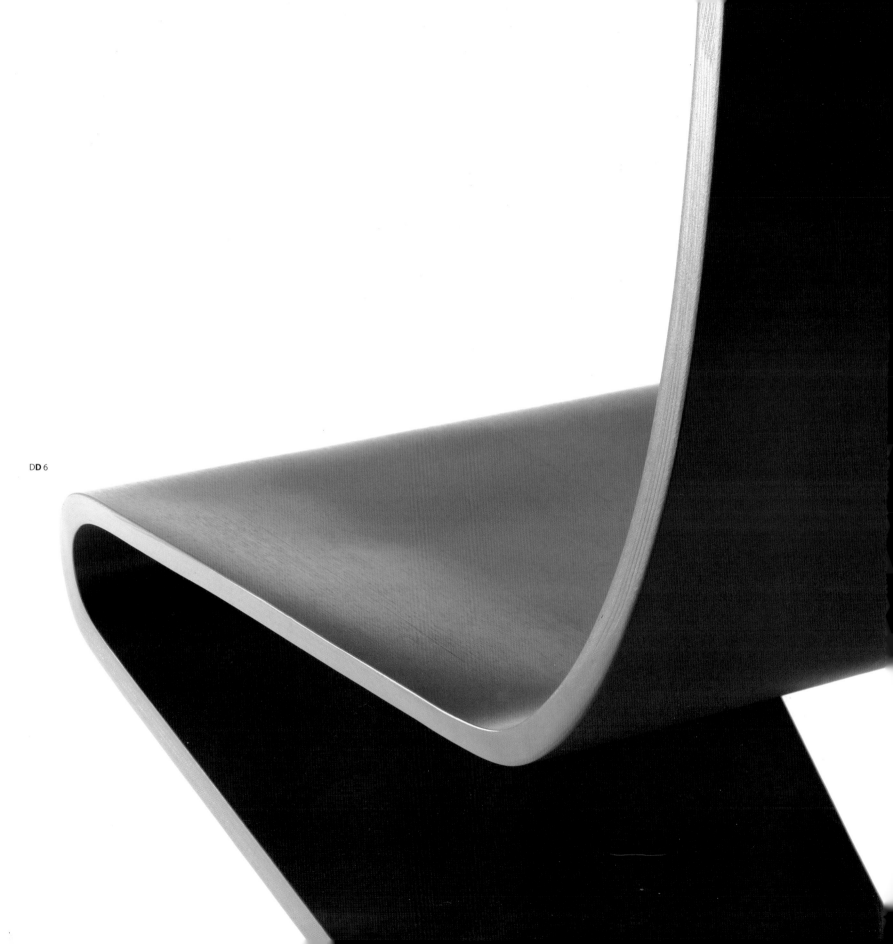

DD 6

# form

In the fourth century B.C., Aristotle defined reality as being made up of entities characterized by consistency of form and matter, where the matter is that which physically composes a thing, and the form is the specific quality of that thing. So, if the balance is changed, it is possible that the change occurs only in the matter (material change), or only in the form (formal change). In an Aristotelian sense, the form is the principle by which we distinguish an entity.

Much later, in the third century A.D., Plotinus became interested in the study of form as a measure of beauty. He followed the Platonic model, rather than Aristotle's, believing that beauty itself was embodied by a form that, like the other Platonic forms, existed only as a concept.

Ever since, multitudes of philosophers have concentrated their efforts on the study of form and its relationship to the sublime in art, on beauty and aesthetics.

In a less philosophical way, an analytic study of the language of visual expression defines various morphological agents of differentiation: form, color, texture, and composition are among the most essential. The study of structural relations between these agents in the visual field shows that each basic organization has meaning in and of itself. The ultimate goal of any good design is an optimal combination of the elements of the composition for a logical equilibrium of visual sensations. It is the method of demonstrating effectively the significance of the whole; it is the capacity to transmit a message to the viewer using psychological aspects of human perception and the cultural connotations of certain elements.

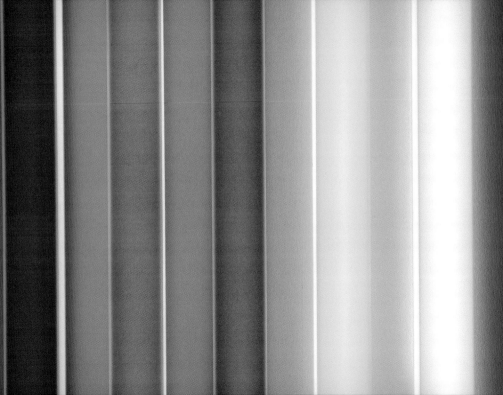

# color

Considering the basic idea that color in itself does not exist, color's importance consists in our subjective appreciation of the sensation produced on the human organ of vision by rays of light. For some designers, color is one of the most personal methods of expression, given that it can create a feeling of attraction or rejection according to its use. Color can move a viewer, invoking emotions and sentiments. It is crucial to the success of a design. To speak in the "language of colors" is to play upon the psychology of color, the different ambiances that can be suggested: calm, happiness, or violence.

Though Goëthe is now commonly considered mainly as a great poet, he was known in his own time as a scientist, and among his many contributions was an intensive study of the effects of color on individuals. Today, this study still provides an important fount of information in this area. Brilliantly, he deduced that hot colors were stimulants, producing happiness or excitement, whereas cold colors were associated with tranquility, sedation, or even depression. Even though these were purely subjective determinations, many investigations have demonstrated the truth of these unconscious associations within a majority of individuals, bound in some way to diverse associations with natural phenomena.

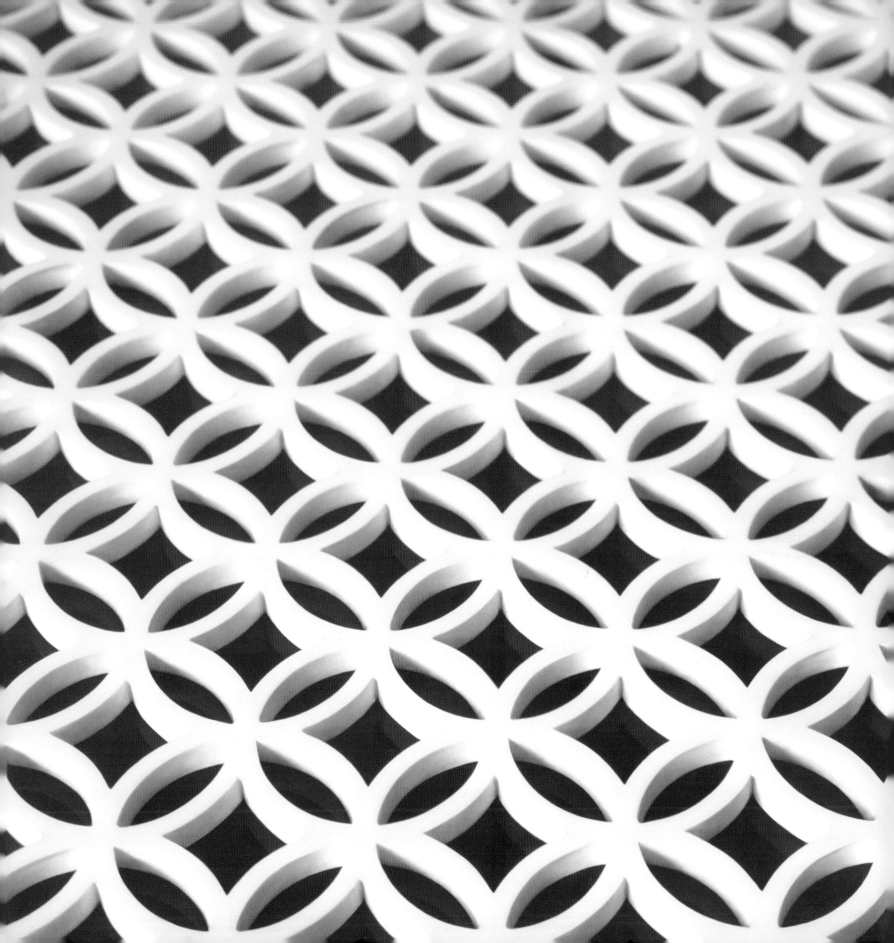

# material

According to Penny Sparke,* innovation in the design of furniture during the twentieth century has been attributed, to varying extents, to a succession of advances in technology. Ever since the widespread use and availability of wood initiated the straight-line tradition, scientific developments have afforded designers opportunities to experiment with new materials. The search for new forms in design has been reflected by the bent-wood chairs made by Thonet in Austria, the bent-steel tables of Le Corbusier, from his "Machines for Living," or the works of Marcel Breuer, also of Thonet's company, made possible by Alvo Aalto's pioneering use of plywood. With particleboard, he was able to achieve greater rigidity without being bound by the constraints of a traditional frame. For their part, plastics introduced new curves with the use of fiberglass, ABS resins, PVC, or polyurethane. Finally, paper and its derivatives have permitted unexpected new uses of old material; paper blended with fabric or plastic gives greater resistance than paper alone.

Nowadays, the possibilities are practically infinite; the mechanisms of science can easily adapt to the ideas of future designers, rather than being restrictive.

*Sparke, Penny (1986). *Furniture: Twentieth-century Design*. Dutton, New York.

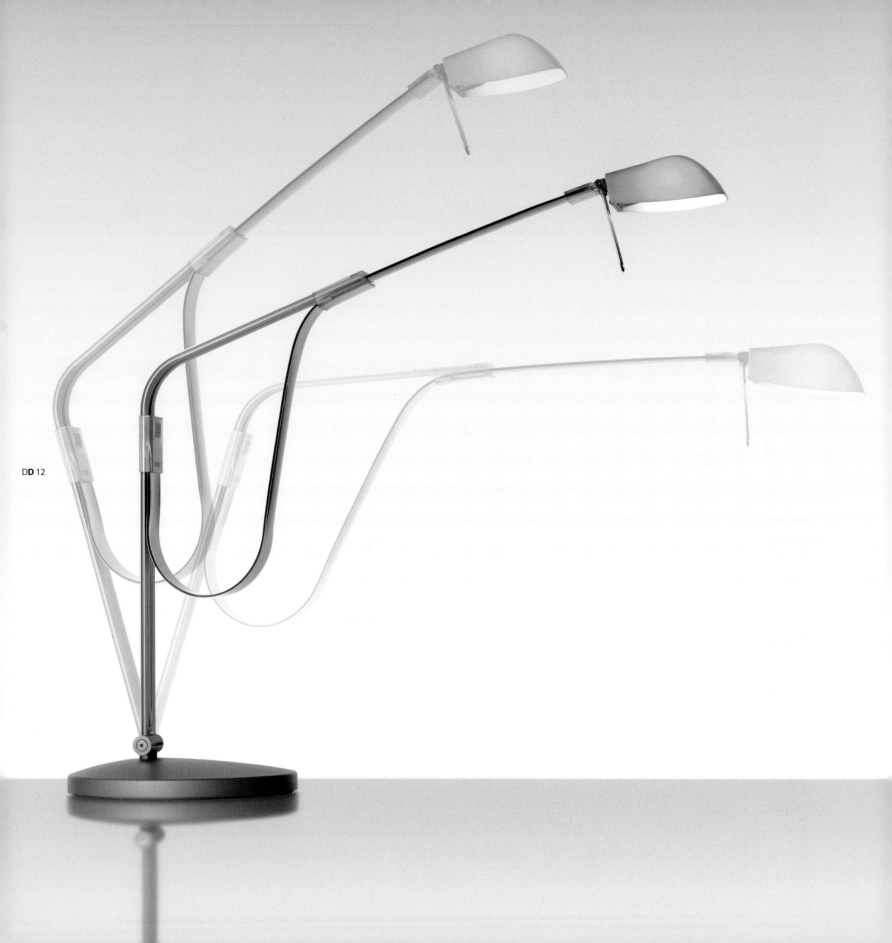

DD 12

# function

To speak about the functionality of design is to speak about the Bauhaus. We are far from the time Walter Gropius founded his school of design, but since then its legacy has continued to influence the character of the work done by so many creators, such as Mies van der Rohe, Le Corbusier, or more recently, Richard Meier, Craig Ellwood, Barbara Barry, Alexander Gorlin, or Philippe Starck.

In 1919, Gropius founded the Bauhaus school in Weimar, Germany, introducing a major innovation to the production aesthetic, fused with the mechanisms of industry. The Bauhaus presented a platform to emphasize the necessity of reforming the pedagogy of art in the service of creating a new type of society. In spite of the changes of location and of direction for the school, one can say that the Bauhaus created the models and established the norms of industrial design as it presently exists. Starting as a school of world art and architecture, and finally arriving as one of the most influential forces in the development of art in the twentieth century, the Bauhaus helped in the invention of modern architecture, and altered the collective consciousness, "from the chair in which you are sitting to the page you are reading." (Wolf Von Eckardt*)

In the manifesto of his foundation, Gropius proposed "architects, painters, and sculptors, we must all return to crafts!" He proposed raising a new form, composed of architecture, sculpture, and painting, "towards the heavens from the hands of a million workers as the crystalline symbol of a new and coming faith."

By commercializing products created with an industrial sensibility, the Bauhaus created a new kind of art object, accessible to the general public.

*van Eckardt, Wolf. "The Bauhaus," in *Horizon, A Magazine of the Arts,* 4:2 (November 1961): 58–75.

DD 14

# design

By definition, design is any activity that leads to the production of a series of beautiful and useful objects. The origin goes back to the Industrial Revolution, the moment when the phases of invention began to separate from the construction of the object itself, establishing marked differences from the traditional system of artisan manufacturing. Even so, it took a while for the major theories to arrive.

The reformist designers of the nineteenth century proposed combining theory and practice, establishing the first bases for the development of the Modernist movement, and the first schools and factories for design. Already at the beginning of the twentieth century, the theories, styles, and philosophies were multiplying.

The complexity inherent in the process of design itself, together with political, socio-economic, cultural, and technological contexts, led to the appearance of design products that could not have existed in any other manner. In this sense, it is good to know the relation between functionalism and periods of economic crisis. By contrast, in times of prosperity, a society tends to dedicate all its efforts to the treatment of superficial issues, to the appearance of the object. But, as happens with everything, the boldest and most applauded designs have been those that proposed solutions to the greatest problems of manufacturers and society in general. This explains the constant flow of new contributions, in the context of the infinite possibilities offered by the ingenuity and creativity of humankind.

DD 16

# innovation

At the moment, the governments of many developed countries are endeavoring to end the constant promotion of the politics of industrial development, enlarging the sphere of multidisciplinary collaborations that propose solutions including many different organizations. In this sense, design has proved an important tool for the development of enterprise, whose success springs from the innovation of its products. Nevertheless, the advancement of current technology has caused an increase in piracy, one of the main problems that, at the moment, limit the creative process.

In 2003, the exhibition "COCO: Copies and Coincidences" opened in Madrid, defending the importance of innovation in design, and having the objective of promoting original creation and taking sensible steps regarding the problem of plagiarism. In this exhibition, the ideas of originality and the right to intellectual property were advanced in response to industries that "take advantage of the risks of others to ensure their own business of copying." According to Juli Capella, it is an attempt to warn that widespread copying could bring about "the end of creation." After all, creation is only possible where there exists a talent able to create true and innovative works of art.

DD 18

# history

It is thought that furniture has existed since the Neolithic age, judging by the samples from Egyptian antiquity where there appear the four essential units: the bed, the chair, the chest, and the table.

Since then, the techniques, motives, styles, and, thus, the pieces themselves have undergone an evolution directly related to the art of the moment, architecture, historical social changes, and, in general, the progress of humanity. Furniture has acquired from its origins a character as functional as it is decorative. From the furniture of a culture, we can interpret and describe its customs, social structure, and the aesthetic model of the time period. In the Roman period of Greece, there existed a kind of U-shaped bed for three people with a table in the center for their food. This was a period of simplicity, where many works were created out of chiseled bronze.

In the Paleo-Christian and Byzantine periods, thrones and beds with canopies began to appear, along with ivory and fine tapestries. In the Romantic period, furniture returned to the massive and heavy. The preponderance of elements pertaining to religion is characteristic of the Gothic period, as is the noticeable vertical element.

In the Renaissance, the atmosphere returned to the more proportional and warm, including the popularization of the armoire and desk. Furniture returned to the horizontal, in pursuit of the serenity of classicalism, and there was an explosion of new techniques. During the Baroque, furniture regained its bulk, and became imposing, tumultuous, and rich. In the culmination of the Rococo style, furniture was characterized by sinuous forms and asymmetry.

During Neoclassicism, the worship of antiquity had retaken straight lines, rested and very geometrical. The form of the imperial, solemn furniture that Napoleon exported to all of Europe had already been seen in Romanticism. Already in the twentieth century, a century of great inventions, there appeared new necessities and new problems, such as the unpublicized difficulties of designers trying not to fit comfortably in any previous style. Plastic artists responded by embracing absolute liberty and true rebellion, finding a new aesthetic that did not depend on the past. They used new materials and experimented with originals made of spare parts, but new inventions, such as the television and computer, were what truly produced a revolution in domestic spaces. What more will change in the twenty-first century?

# furniture

Etymologically, the word *furniture* has its origin in the French *fournir*, meaning "to furnish," although in most European languages, the root is the Latin *mobile*, "movable." Even so, furniture has traditionally done little, as, although movable, it remains static in its uses. Recently the application of new technology has opened new doors in the search for furniture that is much more dynamic and versatile, responding intelligently to human anatomy and to the many needs imposed by society. Ergonomic, adaptable, foldable, portable, washable, inflatable, self-assembling, disposable, recycled…all these words describe elements of design in the last few decades. As an authentic way of showcasing the latest tendencies and realizations in this field, this chapter offers an extensive sampling of the creative minds and personalities who form the recent history of furniture design, such as Xavier Lust, Matali Crasset, Miguel Mila, Theo Williams, and Oscar Tusquets.

22

 **Chair 6** Chair made from two pieces of black-lacquered anodized sheet aluminum. *Xavier Lust*

 **T-Chair** Chair made from one sheet of curved and polished aluminum. *Xavier Lust*

**Ho** This chair has been put together around a single element: a very strong metallic joint that unites the legs, seat, and backrest. The result is an unusual chair that is solid but light and attractive. It is available in cherry, natural oak, gray oak, or wengé. *Luca Meda*

**Sigma** Chaise lounge with square-section chromed metal frame and wooden seats with completely removable fabric or leather covers. The padding, made from double density polyurethane, leaves the border uncovered, revealing the essential design of the profile. Framework in natural oak, gray oak, or wengé. *Hannes Wettstein*

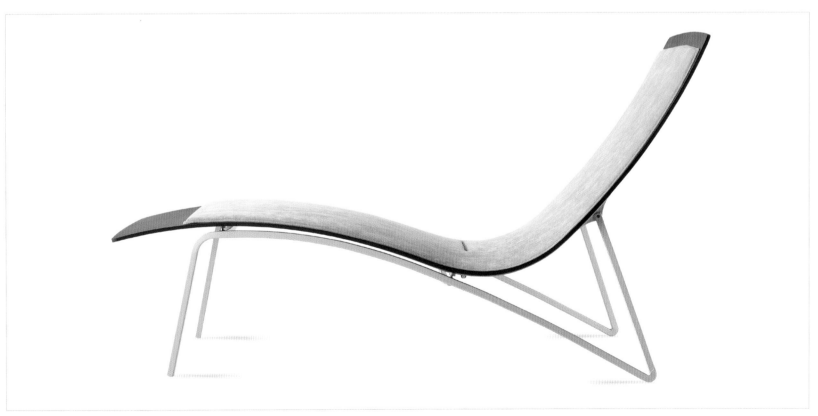

●○
○○ **La Table Basse** Low table made from one piece of curved and folded anodized aluminum with a natural finish. *Xavier Lust*

○●
○○ **Davos Table** Low table with chromed steel frame and wooden top, lacquered in white. *Theo Williams*

●●
○○ **Buismeubel** Low table made from steel tubes attached lengthwise. Available in chrome or white lacquer. *Chris Slutter*

**Quintet** Shelving manufactured from a single piece of aluminum, characterized by a repeating geometric form. The piece can be used to separate spaces, or as a bookcase. *Aziz Sariyer*

●● **Halo** Simple stool made from a curved piece of polypropylene, intriguing from any angle. Lacquered in white. *Intoto*

●● **Pianonotte** Small table supported by a steel tube structure varnished with silver epoxy powder, and finished in eggshell or matte nickel. The top, which includes a drawer, is available in ash, cherry, oak, or matte white lacquer. *Zed*

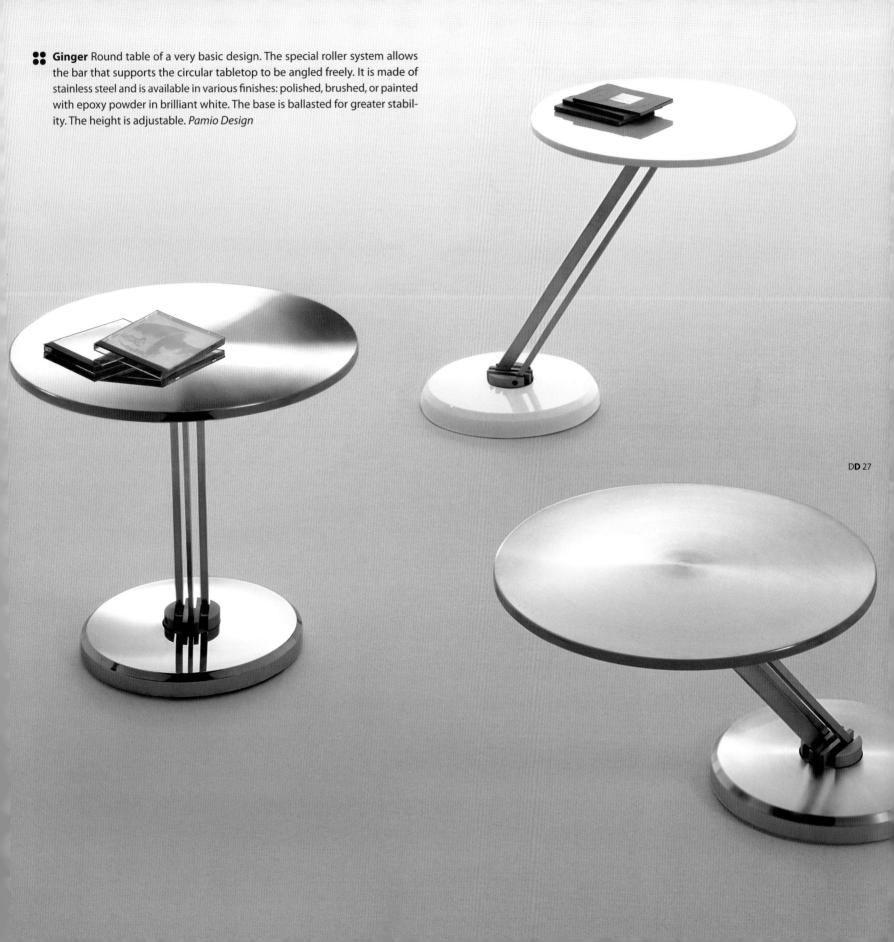

**Ginger** Round table of a very basic design. The special roller system allows the bar that supports the circular tabletop to be angled freely. It is made of stainless steel and is available in various finishes: polished, brushed, or painted with epoxy powder in brilliant white. The base is ballasted for greater stability. The height is adjustable. *Pamio Design*

**Apollo** Armchair with steel frame and moldable foam seat upholstered in fabric or leather. Available with one leg or four in chromed metal. *Patrick Norguet*

**La Grande Table** Table made from one piece of curved anodized aluminum sheet in a natural finish. Available in three different lengths. *Xavier Lust*

 **Le Banc** Bench made from a single piece of curved anodized aluminum in a natural finish or lacquered in white or red. Available in three different lengths. *Xavier Lust*

**Ribbon** Chair of singular design with a metal frame and horizontal springs covered in foam and fabric. The leg is lacquered metal shaped like a pedestal. *Pierre Paulin*

:: **Witch** This series of chairs came about as the result of an investigation into new and different ways of covering chairs. These pieces are upholstered with strips of hanging leather. *Tord Boontje*

**Cloudy Night** This bed has a perimeter in curved laminate, with finishes in lacquered matte white, aluminum, natural American walnut, and oak stained dark gray. The frame is made from square-section stainless steel with a brushed finish. The mattress support is laminate finished with non-toxic water-based matte white lacquers. *Kazuhiro Yamanaka*

DD 31

 **Continua** Metal containers varnished with epoxy powder in titanium or white. The doors, backs, and drawer fronts are in wood lacquered to match the matte colors on the containers. The containers are on casters. *Zed*

**Phoenix** Table with a steel support and wooden top painted in varying colors. *Patricia Urquiola*

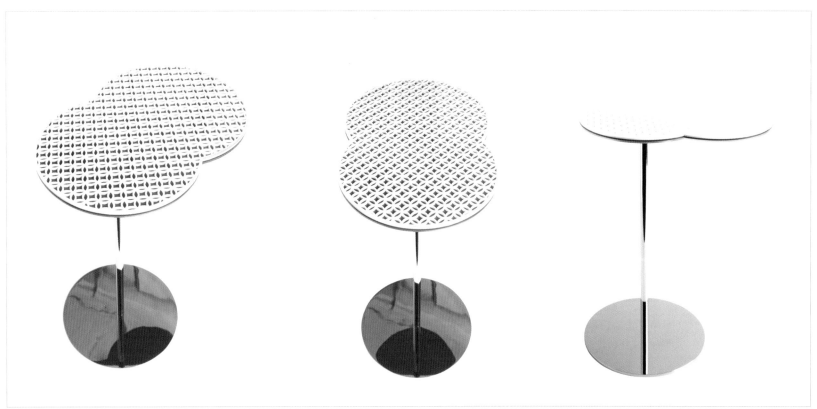

•• **Motif** Table with resistant acrylic polycarbonate top and polished stainless steel legs. *Intoto*

•: **Regal** This piece of furniture is made of oak wood. It is a combination of modular pieces that can be used as a bench, a small table, or a bookcase. *Sandra Lindner*

●● **Take Off** Armchair with steel frame covered in polyester foam. There is also
●● a version with an adjustable base and legs. *Alfredo Häberli*

■■ **Jefferson** Stool with seat made of black rubber and legs of chromed steel.
■■ *Alexander Lervik*

**S 411** Armchair with chromed steel frame and seat and backrest of fabric- or leather-upholstered foam. *Thonet*

**Aline** Sofa with a solid varnished steel frame and legs. The piece can be purchased in several standard colors or in any custom color. *Gregor Schürpf*

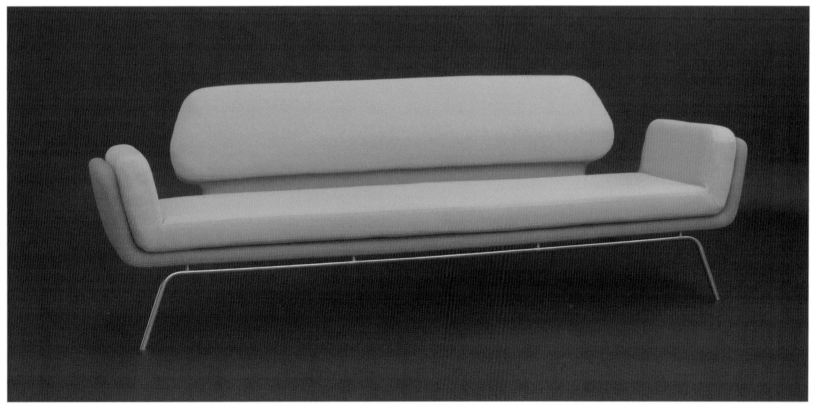

DD 36

**Diva** Bar stool made of polyethylene and available in different colors. The footrest is in chromed stainless steel. *Büro Für Form*

 **Basilea** Armchair with built-in table for comfortable working. The table is available in wood or leather. *John and Samatha Ritschl-Lassoudry*

 **Rotor** Small lounge table with rotating leaves for small and large spaces, for few or many guests. The first and last leaves are fixed, while the central three rotate 360° to create a variety of forms. Available in wengé, bleached oak, ebony, white laminate with edges in wengé, or Acrilux red, white, or gray with edges in bleached oak. *Luciano Bertoncini*

∷ **Flight** Chair made from one sheet of curved steel, lacquered in white. *Büro Für Form*

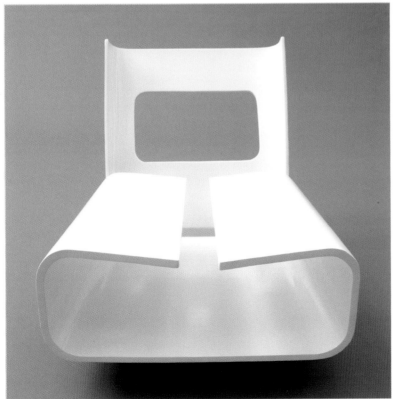

●● **Il Crollo** Design chair made entirely from wood and lacquered in white. The most charming characteristic is the jaunty positioning of the backrest. *Büro Für Form*

●● **Rocker** Chair with wooden frame and leather-upholstered foam. The seat and backrest have the same symmetry. The piece does not have legs. *Büro Für Form*

●● **Stoel** Armchair with curved one-piece aluminum frame lacquered in white. *Chris Slutter*

●● **Ludwig** The front panel and part of the top of this container open simultaneously. The door is made of an ultra-light porous material with the same finish as the top. The interior and back panel are in white lacquered wood and laminate. The top comes in gray oak, brown oak, ash oak, or ebony. *Lodovico Acerbis*

●● **Tolo** Sofas with wooden structures covered in foam and polyester. Cushions for the seat are polylatex covered in pressed and aged polyester fiber. Backrest cushions are polylatex and fiber flakes covered in polyester fiber. The suspension system is based on elastic bands. The wooden legs are in wengé-colored ash. *Rafemar*

■■ **Tic** Swivel chair with padded steel frame, upholstered in leather. The base is made from chromed steel and finished in the form of a cross. *Rafemar*

● ● **Swing** Hammock made of pieces of teak wood cut and covered in neoprene. It can be folded for easy transportation. *Matthias Demacker*

● ● **Caterpillar** Hammock made from steel tubing covered in neoprene. *Matthias Demacker*

**Century** Glass display case with chromed steel frame and fitted halogen lamp. *Alberto Danese*

**Wang** Simple table in solid wood. The sides are the same width as the thickness of the table, lending it a harmonious balance and perfect symmetry. *Gijs Papvoirle*

**Hi** Hat stand made from polished aluminum with base and bar in metal with a silver varnish. There is also a bar for umbrellas, in the same material as the stand. *Fiedeler and Raasch*

**Paso Doble** Umbrella stand with a curved form in red polyethylene. *Xavier Lust*

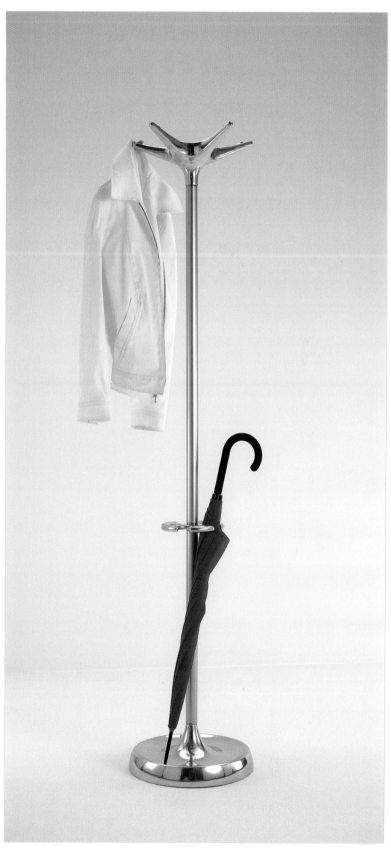

DD 46

 **Cobra** Coffee table available with either one or two transparent glass tops, wooden leg in ash, and chromed stainless steel base. *Cà Nova Design*

 **Meridian** Bookcase in white lacquered wood with chromed steel legs. *Nencini & Brothers*

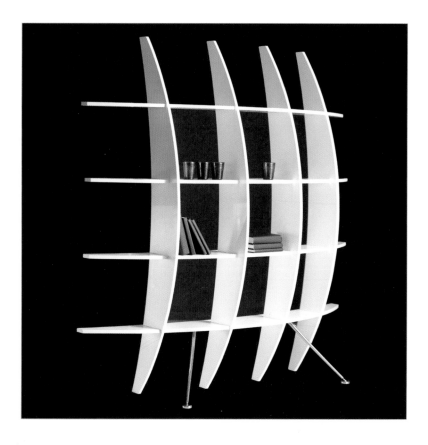

●● **Lounge** Chair with metal frame; seat and backrest are in foam upholstered in wool. The legs are chromed. *Alexander Lervik*

●● **Bar Chair** Bar chair with chromed steel tube legs and seat in black rubber. There is a small opening in the backrest for better handling. *Molteni*

**Hara** Armchair in polyethylene reinforced with lacquered fiberglass.
*Kundalini*

DD 49

**Dip** Small armchair with rounded lines made from polyurethane foam upholstered in wool. The leg is in chromed metal, and the base is of the same material, lacquered to match the upholstery. *Ashley Hall*

**Opium** Hammock with aluminum frame covered by a small, thin molded wooden mat. An extending system allows the piece to fold up or be fully opened as needed. *Fuseproject*

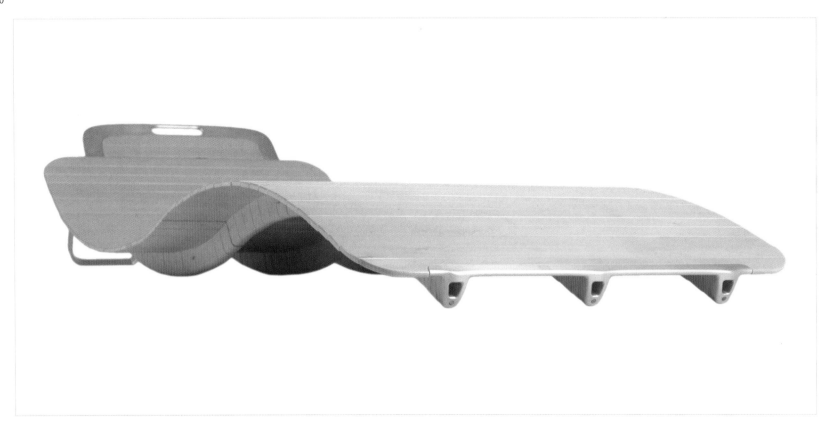

•• **Driade** Chair with chromed stainless steel legs; seat and backrest in polypropylene. The chair can be hooked onto others of the same model by the back, thanks to the openings in its sides. The piece can be used indoors or outdoors. *Shaun Fynn*

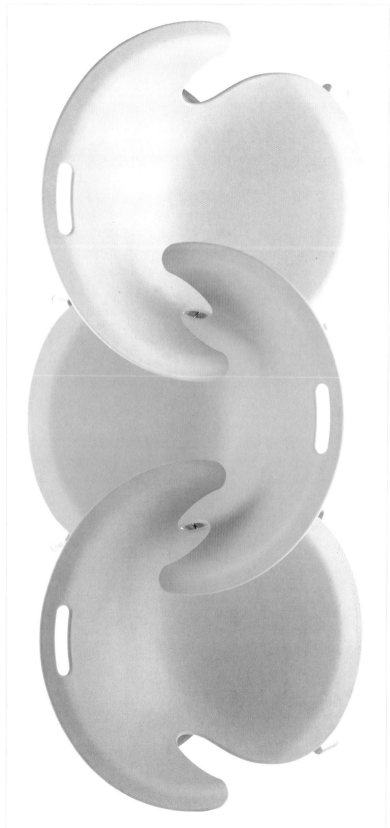

**Tower** Bookcase that rotates over a shaft. The wooden shelves are lacquered in either white or black. The shaft and base are in chromed steel. *Studio Diapason*

**Statica** This bookcase allows the customer to arrange the shelves according to his or her taste—top to bottom, left to right. A beam to fix the piece to the wall or ceiling is included. *Daniele Lago*

**Jet** Coffee table made of a single piece of polished stainless steel.
*Giorgio Cattelan*

DD 53

**Lovecage** Bed with perimeter, headboard, footrest, and legs in anodized aluminum with a natural finish. The legs can be set at two heights. The bed base is made of wooden slats held together by rubber. *Giovanni Levanti*

**Valeria** Swivel chair with seat in brilliant fiberglass and base in chromed steel. *Büro Für Form*

**Teatro** Chair in natural oak, gray oak, wengé, or brilliant black or white lacquer. The rigor and precision of the design is softened by the attention to detail, the curves, and the padded surfaces. The padding of the seat and backrest is made from polyurethane covered in fabric or leather. *A. Rossi and L. Meda*

**Marais Daybed** Daybed fitted with an internal mechanism, activated by remote control, that provides a soft vibration to massage the whole body or specific zones. The base is finished in brilliant aluminum. The cover, in fabric or leather, is completely removable. *Paola Navone*

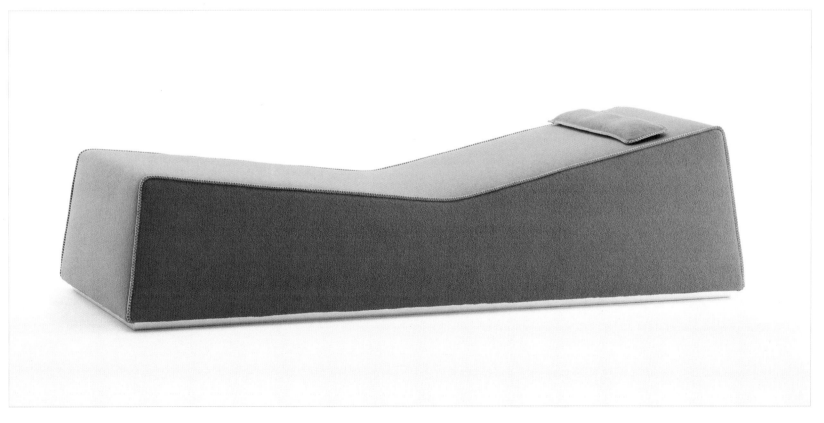

●■ **Smalltown** Armchair with wooden frame and backrest; seat in cold foam and
■■ nonflammable fibers upholstered in fabric or leather. Legs in chromed or lacquered metal. *Eero Koivisto*

■● **Midtown** Armchair with wooden structure filled with foam and nonflam-
■■ mable fibers, upholstered in fabric or leather. The legs are chromed steel
tube. *Eero Koivisto*

**Easy Block** Sofa with wooden frame with base, backrest, and seat in fire-proof cold foam upholstered in fabric. The legs are in chromed or silver metal. The sofa can be separated into two pieces of different colors. *Jean-Marie Massaud*

DD 57

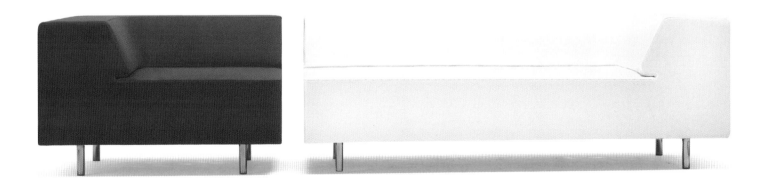

●● **Alba** Chair with seat and backrest veneered in natural wood, stained, or lacquered. The legs are in chromed metal. Also available with the seat upholstered in fabric or leather. *Marten Claesson*

■■
■● **Queen** Armchair with backrests and seat in molded cold foam and base in Pullmaflex upholstered in fabric or leather. The legs are in chromed or silvered metal, and the armrests are in wood, birch, or oak, upholstered in leather. *Olle Anderson*

**Doppio** Sofa and chair suite without arms, with wooden frame filled with cold foam and upholstered in leather. The legs are steel tubes. *Eero Koivisto*

DD 60

●● **Lagoon** Coffee table with low top in opaque glass and high top in transparent glass. The base is in chromed stainless steel. *Giorgio Manzali*

●● **Librería** Bookcase in steel lacquered in white and black. The shelves are in metal of the same color. *Patricia Urquiola*

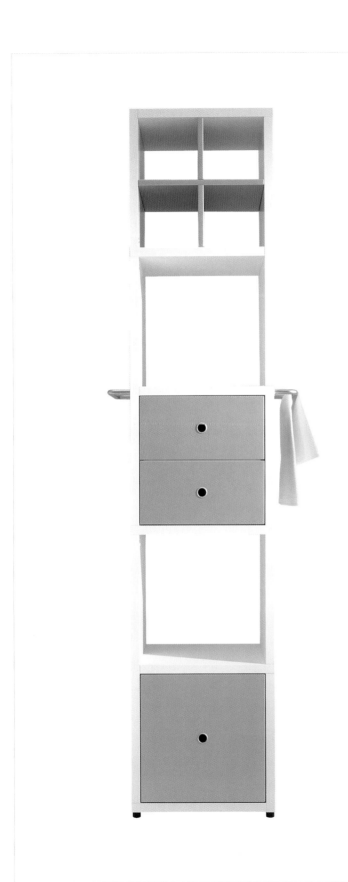

● ◦
◦ ◦ **Freddy** Bookcase for the bathroom in lacquered wood with stainless steel bars on the sides and drawers in two sizes. The legs are in steel with rubber pads. *Hertel Klarhoefer*

◦ ●
◦ ◦ **Freddy** This variation is made from the same materials, with the exception of the legs, which are chromed steel tubing. *Hertel Klarhoefer*

⣿ **Otto** Armchair made from one piece of wood lined with fabric in the center. The opening in the interior also serves as a storage space. *John Greg Ball*

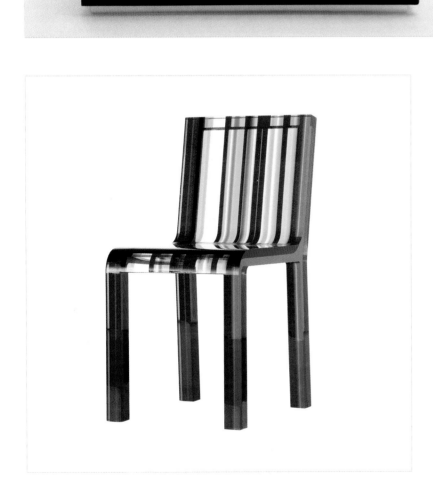

**Marais** Collection of sofas and armchairs characterized by their pyramid profiles. All of the bases are finished in brilliant aluminum. The covers, either in fabric or leather, are completely removable. *Paola Navone*

**Rainbow** Chair made entirely from colored panels of acrylic glass. *Patrick Norguet*

**Little Apollo** Chair with seat made from wood, covered in foam and upholstered in fabric. The legs are molded chromed steel tube. *Patrick Norguet*

**Orly** Sofa with wooden frame upholstered in fabric. The chromed steel tube legs are set in the frame. *Patrick Norguet*

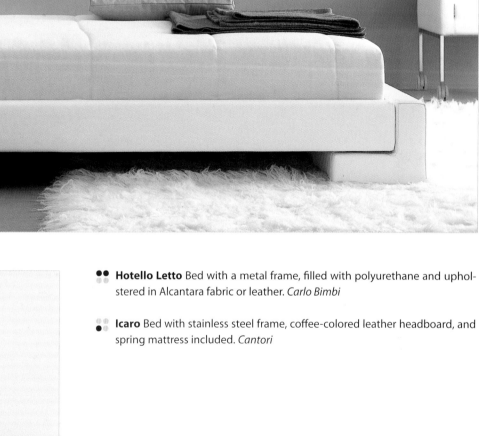

DD 65

 **Hotello Letto** Bed with a metal frame, filled with polyurethane and upholstered in Alcantara fabric or leather. *Carlo Bimbi*

**Icaro** Bed with stainless steel frame, coffee-colored leather headboard, and spring mattress included. *Cantori*

**Sky** Console table with chromed metal frame and white lacquered aluminum top. *Andy Ray*

**Sax** Low lightweight chromed aluminum table on wheels. *ClassiCon*

**Regal** Wall mirror with opaque glass frame. *Giorgio Cattelan*

**Palco** Rotating unit for plasma TV with stainless steel shaft and base, and shelves in transparent glass. *Emanuele Zenere and Alberto Danese*

DD 67

● ● **Boson** Armchair with base in white lacquered steel and seat in quilted synthetic material. *Patrick Norguet*

● ● **Prime Time** Set of two chairs, inversely oriented, made from one sheet of chromed aluminum, with wooden rocking base. *Afroditi Krassa*

**Void** Armchair of molded sheet birch with interior in white laminated wood and legs in polished stainless steel. *Intoto*

**Lex** Ergonomic sofa of minimalist design, with stainless steel frame and leather upholstery. The legs are chromed steel tubes. *Patrick Norguet*

**Spritz** Coffee table with sliding top, which opens onto a storage space. The frame of the sides and base is polished stainless steel, and the top is painted black glass with mirrors. *Cá Nova Design*

●● **Phoenix** These containers are made out of aluminum and sheets of wood in
●● a natural finish. *Patricia Urquiola*

●● **Icaro** Coffee table with double top: the lower piece is tinted black glass and the
●● higher, in transparent glass, rotates. The axle is chromed steel. *Marino Burba*

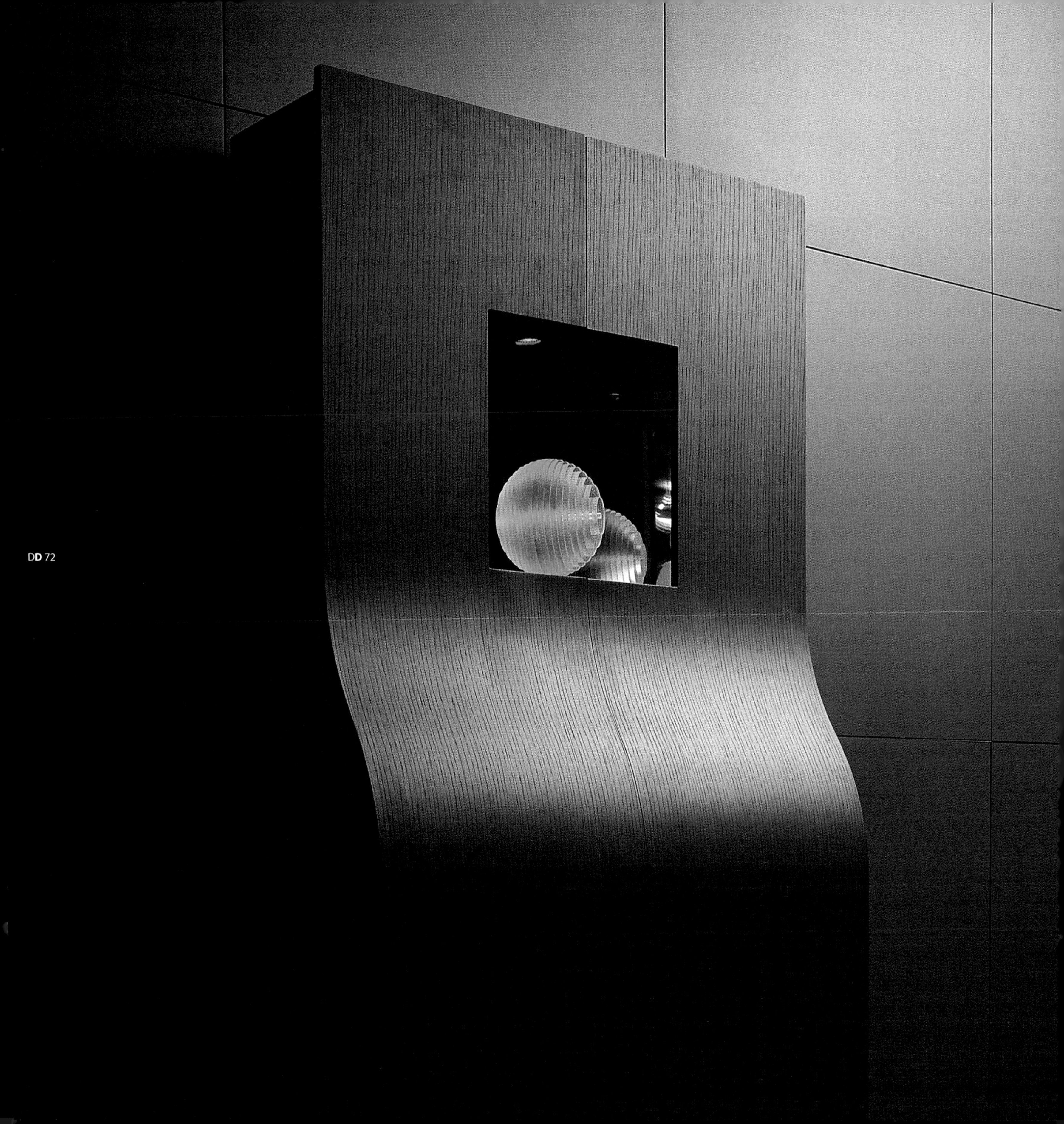

DD 72

**Sinus** Vertical sideboard characterized by two different depths in its interior and exterior. Its undulating doors, in laminate finished in gray oak or lacquered in black or red, are highly polished on both faces. The doors, which are detachable, have special hinges and a rotating arm in varnished metal. The top is gray laminated wood. *Pepe Tanzi*

**Digitspace** Hexagonal ottomans that can be put together in different shapes to create original pieces. They are polyurethane foam covered in fabric and high-resistance melamine. *Matali Crasset*

**Panther** This chair can also be used as a sofa if tipped over. It has a fiberglass frame upholstered in velvet. *Satyendra Pakhalé*

● ● **Horse Chair** Chair in the shape of a horse, with large backrest for greater comfort. The fiberglass frame is upholstered in velvet. *Satyendra Pakhalé*

● ● **Bird** Chaise lounge made of fiberglass and upholstered in velvet, with chromed aluminum base. *Satyendra Pakhalé*

 **Lukum** Two-seater sofa with wooden frame covered in polyurethane foam and upholstered in completely removable polyester. The two pieces can be used separated or linked together. *Patricia Urquiola*

 **Solichair** Wooden-framed armchair with backrest and seat in cold foam upholstered with fabric or leather. Metal base in either chromed or silvered metal. *Alfredo Häberli*

**Horse Chair** Chair in the shape of a horse, with a large backrest. It is made of fiberglass covered with coconut yarn. *Satyendra Pakhalé*

●● **Hotello Daybed** This combination daybed-chair offers maximum relaxation.
●● The metal frame is filled with polyurethane and upholstered in either Alcantara
fabric or leather. *Carlo Bimbi*

●● **Dual** Table with top in wood veneer or lacquered in white. *Eero Koivisto*
●●

**Comé** This series of low cabinets includes units of drawers, cupboards, and open shelves, as well as bedside tables. Available in natural beech, whitened beech, mocha stain, or cherry. *Studio Técnico Horm*

**Tangram** The idea of this shelving system for books is based on and named after the Chinese geometry game. *Daniele Lago*

●● **Orit** Reclining chair, comfortable in any position. The base is chromed
●● steel, and the foam support is covered in removable flexible leather.
*Siegfried Bensinger*

●● **Fly Chair** Chair with chromed steel tube frame and legs in thicker steel with
●● matte varnish. *Teppo Asikainen*

**Monoeast** Armchair with wooden frame filled with cold foam and upholstered in fabric. The chromed steel legs support the seat and the backrest.

**F-Seat** Sofa with wooden frame; backrest and seats in cold nonflammable foam upholstered in fabric. The base is chromed metal. *Thomas Eriksson*

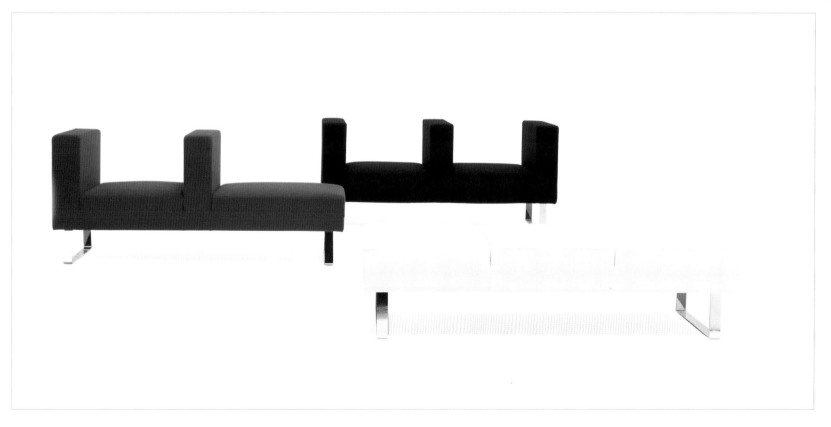

**Three Skin** Chair with extremely pronounced lines—more sculpture than chair. It is made of lacquered wood. *Ron Arad*

**Lounge** Sofa with steel frame and cold polyurethane foam form. Base in chromed or aluminum-painted steel. The upholstery, in fabric or leather, covers the entire sofa and can be completely removed. *Xavier Lust*

**Davos** Series of beds and sofas with wooden frames in natural finishes or lacquered in white. The legs are chromed stainless steel and may be concealed by a wooden skirt. *Theo Williams*

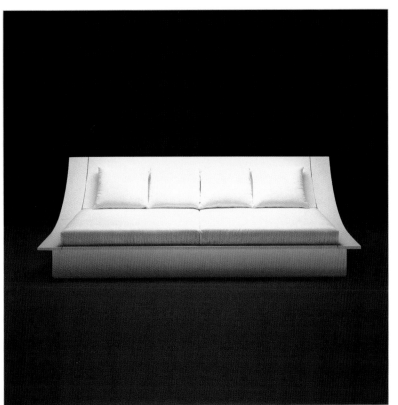

●● **2020** Series of elegant containers with drawers and folding or detachable
●● doors. The exterior is available in three finishes: natural oak, gray oak, or
wengé. In the interior, removable shelves lacquered in a mineral green color
can be fitted. The units may be supported on legs or mounted on the wall.
The series can be used in the living room as console tables or in the bedroom
as chests of drawers. *Studio F & L*

●● **Joseph** Group of three small tables that can be used in different positions,
●● thanks to the folded top. The anodized aluminum frame can be combined
with a top of the same material with borders in wengé, or with a wooden top
in natural oak, gray oak, or wengé. *Hannes Wettstein*

**Freddy Lack** Wooden bookcase lacquered and varnished in different colors.
*Hertel Klarhoefer*

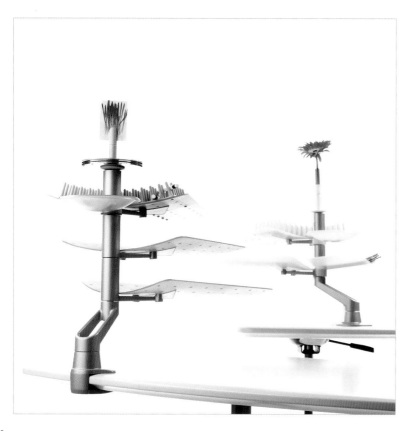

●● **Desk Top** This writing desk organizer consists of a rotating steel arm with clamp or grommet mount to attach it to the table. The small movable tables come in different colored hard plastics. *Shaun Fynn*

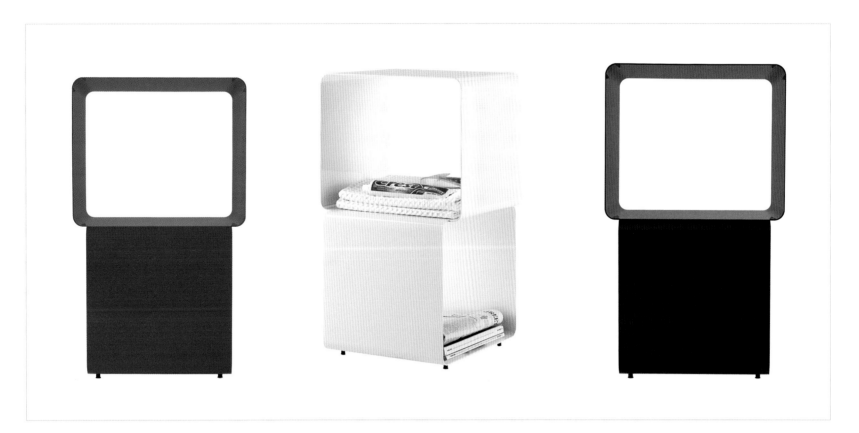

 **Dadi** Two open-sided cubes form a multipurpose unit, available in steel lacquered in red, white, or black. *Gianluigi Landoni*

 **Carrello** Painted stainless steel trolley for stacking and transporting folding chairs. Fitted with wheels. *Giorgio Cattelan*

●● **Trends** This is a new series of the famous "Tam-Tam" stools. The models shown here are: Hula Hoop, Ondulation, and Ting Tang. *Henry Massonnet*

●● **Scoop** Service tables and auxiliary tables in marine board finished in cherry, natural oak, gray oak, and matte white lacquer. The frame is steel varnished with silver-colored epoxy powder. *Mesh Design*

**Ripple** Injection-molded plastic chair with legs in varnished steel. *Ron Arad*

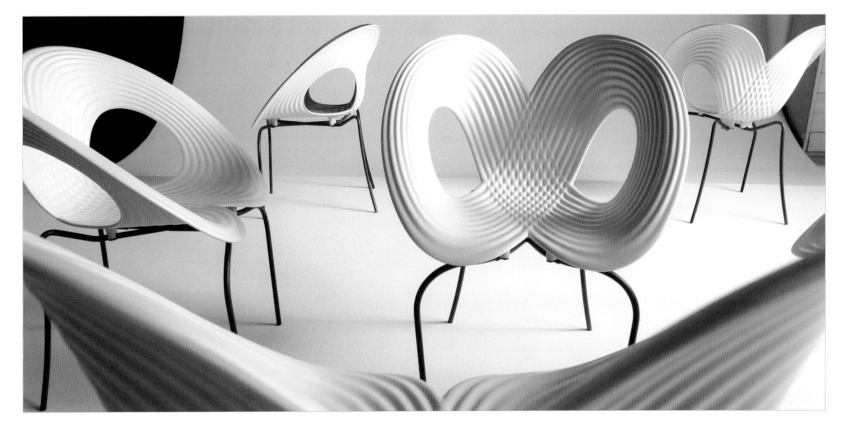

**Stilo** The supporting frame, brackets, and handles of this modular container are in stainless anodized aluminum with fronts, doors, and drawers in stainless steel, either brushed or matte, or lacquered in matte white, light gray, or intense red. *Carlo Tamborini*

● ● **Alto** Container with frames available in aluminum, natural ash, bleached ash,
● ○ mocha-stained ash, cherry-stained ash, and sandblasted or tempered glass.
*Studio Técnico Horm*

● ● **Jeff** Adaptable, functional armchair with foam-filled seat and armrests uphol-
● ○ stered in leather. The chromed aluminum base rotates. *Johannes Foersom and
Peter Hiort-Lorenzen*

● ● **Swan** Extendable dining room table with frosted glass top and wooden legs
● ○ in wengé or bleached oak. *Andy Ray*

●● **Violona** Chair with a high backrest and a metal frame completely upholstered in leather, available in different colors. *Piero de Longhi*

●● **Unic** Armchair with a cold polyurethane structure and a stainless steel base with brushed finish. Removable or permanent coverings are available in fabric and leather. *Zed*

●● **Viva** Office chair with adjustable inclination and height. The rubber seat is upholstered in fabric, and the legs are made from chromed steel tube. *Komplot*

●● **Collage** Chair with molded aluminum frame and foam upholstered in fabric. The armrests become the legs in a curve running from top to bottom. *Komplot*

**Waiter-Waitress** The elements of this two-piece multipurpose system can be used individually or together, allowing for great diversity. *Formstelle*

**Skan** Container with glass doors and sides. The frame is matte white lacquered chipboard, and the top and profiles are aluminum, with adjustable legs. It is available with either two or three sandblasted glass shelves and lamps. *Studio Técnico Horm*

● ● **Modern** This new series of multipurpose pieces uses special refined thick
wooden panels to support televisions and other hi-fi components. The wood
is finished with a special coffee-colored veneer. *Piero Lissoni*

● ● **Taolino** Antique-style bedside table made from a single piece of curved iron.
The drawer is in a coffee-colored leather. *Cantori*

●● **Valentinonox** Dining room table with a stainless steel base and supporting ball in light-colored marble. The top is transparent glass. *Emanuele Zenere*

●● **Coco** Oval-shaped table in cherry or oak, finished in cherry, wengé, or oak colors, or lacquered in white, gray, or red. The base is metal. *Rafemar*

• **Coco Redonda** Set of round cherry or oak tables of different heights, finished in cherry, wengé, or oak colors, or lacquered in white, gray, or red. The base is metal. *Rafemar*

• **Io** Freestanding mirror with varnished natural wood frame. *Rafemar*

⠞ **Orbit** Series of seating systems with steel frame filled with molded cold foam and upholstered in fabric. The legs are chromed steel tubes. *Eero Koivisto*

**Flower** Molded cold foam ottomans with polyurethane surfaces. Available in red or orange. *Eero Koivisto*

●● **Solitaire** Armchair with wooden frame; seat and backrest filled with cold foam and upholstered in fabric or leather. The base is available in chromed or silvered metal. A complementary table is included. *Alfredo Häberli*

●● **Tinto** Armchair with seat and backrest in molded cold foam, upholstered in fabric or leather. The legs are available in chromed or silvered metal. *Claesson Koivisto Rune*

:: **DNA** Series of connectable tables with tops lacquered in white, black, blue, and orange. The base is available in chromed, silvered, or lacquered metal.
*Eero Koivisto*

**Picnik** This combination table-seat was created specially for the terrace, small spaces, and semipublic areas. Made from one piece of curved aluminum and available in five colors. *Xavier Lust*

**Decompression Chair** Ash chair with inflatable polyester fabric piece, which converts the straight-back chair into a very original armchair. *Matali Crasset*

**K-line** Series of accessories in wood veneer and chromed metal. *Khodi Feiz*

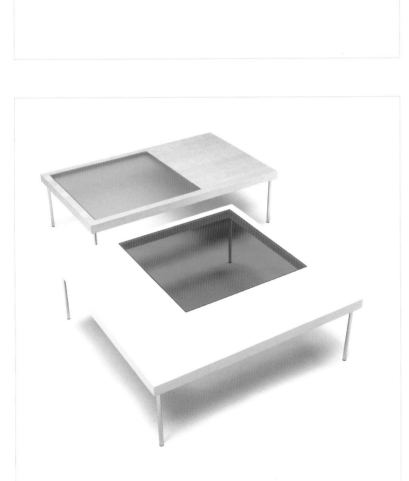

**Pickup** Car-shaped seat with wooden frame; seat and backrest in cold non-flammable foam. The rubber wheels are sunk into the frame. *Alfredo Häberli*

**Tray** Table with natural wood or lacquered white top. The upper tabletop works as a removable tray. The bottom surface of the tray is polyurethane, and the base is chromed metal. *Monica Förster*

**Window** Central table with top finished in wood veneer or white lacquer with red, green, blue, or transparent glass. The legs are available in chromed or silvered metal. *Eero Koivisto*

**Collage** Series of interlocking melamine tables with steel legs. *Komplot*

**Harrys** Table for the kitchen, the garden, or anywhere else in the house. The base is made from an aluminum alloy, and the top is a thick sheet of aluminum. All of the surfaces are polished. *Luciano Bertoncini*

**Lobster** Set of chromed aluminum tables that can be arranged in a variety of configurations. *Komplot*

⣿ **Mushroom** Armchair with steel frame covered in moldable foam. This piece is part of the permanent collection of the Museum of Modern Art in New York. *Pierre Paulin*

**Duplo** This piece is lacquered in an earth tone, and the interior of the cabinet space is in wengé. *Azcue*

**Bitter Duplo** This piece is finished in white lacquer and cherry. It holds three drawers and has a door at the bottom. *Azcue*

**Duplo Roble** A piece with six drawers, finished in natural oak. *Azcue*

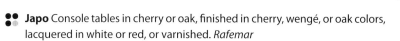 **Japo** Console tables in cherry or oak, finished in cherry, wengé, or oak colors, lacquered in white or red, or varnished. *Rafemar*

DD 114

**Couch** One-seater with ottoman. The wooden frame is completely covered in foam and upholstered in different colored canvas. There is also a loveseat in this series. *Stefan Diez*

**Chill Out** Chaise lounge for a new kind of rest. The metal frame is covered in leather with rollers that make up the upper part of the piece. The legs are chromed metal. *Manfred Wakolbinger*

⠿ **Air** Molded chrome ceiling hanger with steel cable, weighted for better stability. *A. Quaggiotto, Pio and Tito Toso*

⠿ **Dodici** Cactus-shaped clothes stand in steel, varnished with epoxy powder and finished in white, orange, and silver. *James Irvine*

**Hang It** Hanger manufactured in fiberglass and colored. The piece is hung from the ceiling with a polished aluminum fixing. *Olaf Kitzig*

**Oka** Clothes rack available in two versions. One hangs from the ceiling and the other stands on the floor. The first hangs from a steel wire and moves. The other has steel legs and a base of the same material. The hooks are in polyurethane and available in different colors. *Teppo Asikainen*

**Classic** Armchair with tubular steel frame and horizontal bar upholstered in moldable foam. *Pierre Paulin*

DD 118

 **Isobel** Sofa with removable cushions in the armrests that make the piece solid or open. *Michel Van der Kley*

 **Butterfly** Armchair with frame in stainless steel and seat in the shape of a harness, available in black or natural leather. *Pierre Paulin*

**Flyt** Series of all-purpose ergonomic chairs that stand out for their versatility. Available with or without armrests and with either four legs or a curved base. The frame is aluminum, and the seats are plastic and can be upholstered. The armrests are aluminum covered in a rubbery non-slip material. *C.D.N.*

**Ottoman** Simple, functional piece that can transform from ottoman to chaise lounge. *Matthew Hilton*

DD 122

**Stokke Tok** Reclining armchair with a sophisticated mechanism for smooth changes of position. Its frame consists of three shells in laminated wood over bases of the same material. The chair can be upholstered in soft fabrics or leather. *Toshiyuki Kita*

●● **Swan** Polyurethane sofa reinforced with fiberglass, with seat and backrest in cold foam that is upholstered in fabric or leather. The legs are strips of molded aluminum screwed to the base. *Arne Jacobsen*

●● **PK 31** Two- or three-seater sofa with steel structure covered in leather. The base is made of chromed steel. *Paul Kjaerholm*

**A 660** Swivel chair with a low, chromed steel leg. The seat and backrest have a wooden frame covered with plastic wickerwork. *James Irvine*

**PK 80** Chaise lounge with large mattress in cold foam, upholstered in leather, and folding sides. The legs are stainless steel. *Paul Kjaerholm*

**Skate** Armchair with steel frame filled with fireproof polyurethane foam. The base is PVC. *Alfredo Häberli*

**Sinus** Chaise lounge with steel frame; the seat and backrest have rounded upholstered elements held in place by leather straps in brown or black. The chair rocks, due to the shape of the base. *Reinhold Adolf, Hans Jürgen Schröpfer*

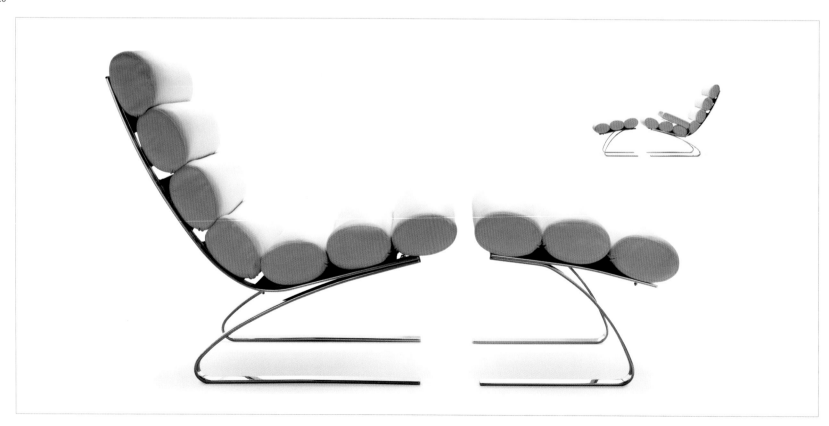

●● **Bloomy** Sofa with steel frame, filled with fireproof polyurethane foam. The legs are polypropylene. *Patricia Urquiola*

●● **Lukum** Small mattress filled with cold foam, upholstered in leather, with foldable backrest. *Patricia Urquiola*

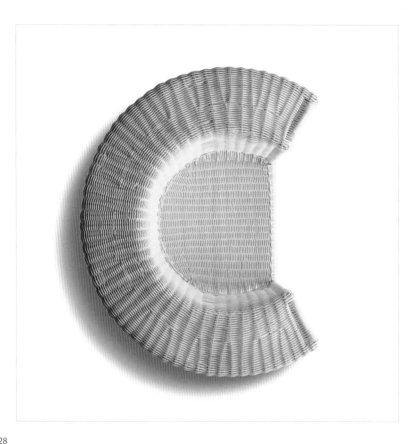

**Charlotte** Armchair with metal frame covered in natural unvarnished rattan. *Mario Botta*

**Line** Chaise lounge in curved laminate with bleached and varnished ash frame and velvet cushion. The footrest can be positioned at different heights. *Carlo Cumini*

**Orbit** Armchair with steel frame; backrest and seat in cold molded foam, upholstered in fabric. The legs are chromed metal. *Eero Koivisto*

**King** Solid, robust chair that combines luxury and comfort. The backrest, the seat, and the rounded armrests are all made of upholstered foam. *Gijs Papavoine*

**⠿ DNA** Bookcase with chromed tubular steel frame in one piece with lacquered wooden shelves and chrome steel legs. *Massimo Iosa Ghini*

:: **Crédence** Anodized aluminum containers lacquered in white or red. Only 150 of these units were manufactured. The interior is in anodized aluminum with a natural finish. *Xavier Lust*

●● **Cornflake** Chair with seat and backrest veneered in natural wood, stained or
lacquered. The legs are available in chromed or silvered metal. Also available
with the seat upholstered in fabric. *Claesson Koivisto Rune*

●●
●○ **Cornflake** Bar chair with seat in white lacquered wood and legs in chromed
steel. *Claesson Koivisto Rune*

**Zentrum** Modular pieces for waiting areas. The series includes sofas, small tables, and benches in two sizes. The frames are chromed aluminum with cushioned seats and backrests. *Biplax*

DD 133

**Quadrivio** One of a series of tables, in different sizes and finishes, that combines simplicity of design with rich, versatile materials. The frame is a single piece of stainless steel with a brilliant finish. The top is available in Carrara marble or glass lacquered in either black or white. *Roberto Monsani*

DD 134

**Airy** Chair with pressed aluminum body, lacquered in white, black, or red. The base is chromed metal, available with four legs or with one rotating leg. The seat is covered in either gray or red velvet or in black horsehide. *Piergiorgio Cazzaniga*

**Ark** Low table with a curved, laminated wood top, over which a second top made of straight glass is inserted. The frame is chromed metal. The table can be disassembled. *Romani-Saccani*

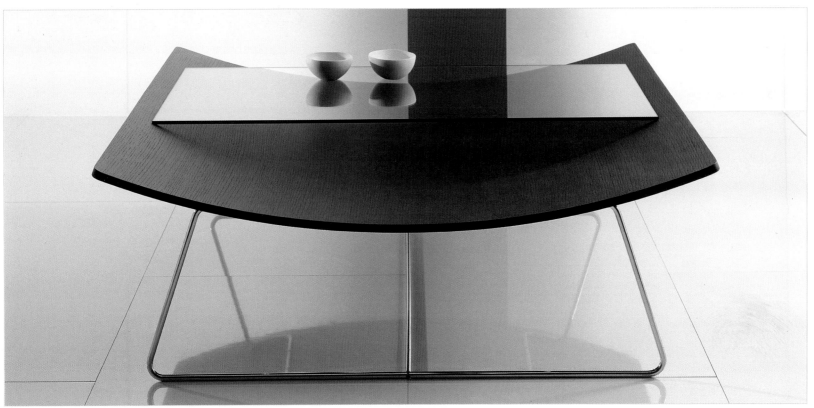

●● **Bordura** Set of cubic containers available in a Macassar ebony finish or lacquered in brilliant white, lead gray, or red. The sides, supporting frame, and handles are all in aluminum. *Luciano Bertoncini*

**El** Bookcase and combination mirror-hanger, both made from stainless steel sheets with back varnished with matte black epoxy powder. The hanger has three pegs, and the bookcase has four fixed shelves. *Laura Agnoletto and Marzio Rusconi Clerici*

●● **Bahamas Alto** Bed with wooden base and headboard covered in removable padded fabric. The mattress rests on wooden panels, and the bed lies on four wooden legs.

●● **VK** Chair made of chromed steel, with seat hand-upholstered in leather. *Burovormkrijgers*

**Ku** Armchair with wooden frame covered in foam. The seat cushion is aged and compacted hollow foam. The seat is suspended on crisscrossed elastic bands. The base is aluminum. *Rafemar*

•• **Giotto** Elegance in soft, rounded lines, aluminum handles, back finishes, innovative drawers, and a wide range of finishes characterize this series of containers and sideboards. Available in natural cherry, natural oak, or lacquered in brilliant white or lead gray. The sides are always lacquered in a silver color. *Team Design*

**Leonardo** This series of containers includes sideboards, display cases, and television stands with horizontal doors that open simultaneously. Available in cherry, dark walnut, Canaletto, or white lacquer. Two of the sideboards are also available in high-gloss white, red, and black lacquers. *Luciano Bertoncini*

●● **Andaman** Tatami-type bed with wooden frame in wengé and dismountable base in coffee-colored wood. *Paola Navone*

●● **Awa** Simple, avant-garde chair with chromed steel tube frame and seat in upholstered high-density polyurethane. The armrests are upholstered in black leather. The chair is stackable. *Biplax*

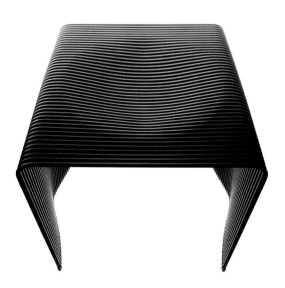

**Soest Stool** Stool, molded from a steel sheet and varnished in black. It is exceptionally comfortable and light. *Mabeg*

**Struc** Stackable chair made of chromed, molded sheet steel. The legs are painted steel. *Mabeg*

**Alternative** Technology and poetry are united in this functional design: a creative, soft, foldable, multipurpose series of tables, available in a variety of woods. The supporting tops are colored, scratch-resistant laminate. *Bernard Vuarnesson*

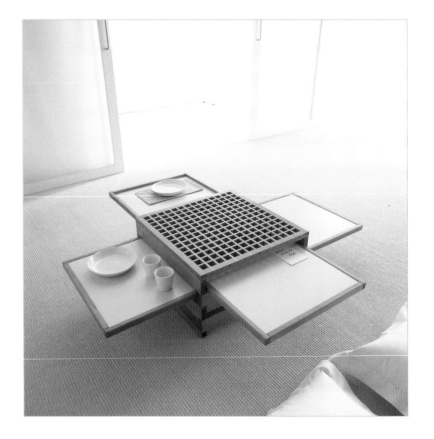

 **Alternative Duo**

**Alternative Hexa**

**Alternative Nuit**

●● **Print** Sofa with wooden frame covered in polyurethane and upholstered in
○○ polyester. The legs are screwed directly onto the frame. *Marcel Wanders*

●● **Hotello Poltron** One-seater sofa with metal frame, filled with polyure-
○● thane and covered in Alcantara fabric or leather. The legs are solid steel.
*Carlo Bimbi*

**S 4000** Suite of sofas and armchairs with folded wooden frames, filled with polyurethane and upholstered in leather. The legs are chromed, molded sheet steel. *Jehs and Laub*

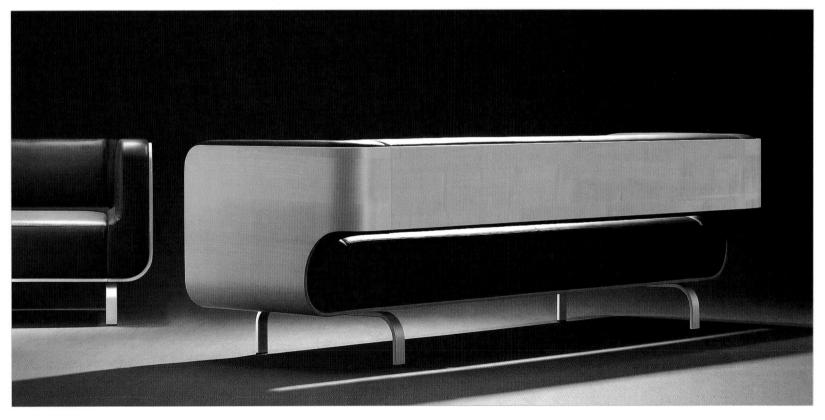

■■ **Axel** Table with chromed stainless steel frame and painted glass top. The table is available with casters; pictured below, the scene is completed with the Vedette chair from the same designer, upholstered in leather over a chromed stainless steel frame. *Andy Ray*

•• **Chat** Armchair with frame in metal filled with cold foam. The base is stainless steel with a brushed finish. Permanent and removable covers are available. *Zed*

•• **Anna** Chair with chromed steel frame, upholstered in soft, padded leather. *Studio Kronos*

**Loft** Sofa with aluminum frame, upholstered in fabric. The seat and backrest are made of foam. The two pieces of the sofa can also be separated. *Paola Piva*

**Speedster** Chair with metal frame, cushioned with nonflammable polyure-thane foam resins. The base is matte brushed stainless steel. The upholstery, in either fabric or leather, can be permanent or removable. *Zed*

**Lima** Sofa system designed with straight lines and rectangular forms. The line of the seams enhances the cubic form of the backrest, seat, and armrests. Combining different elements from the series offers a variety of forms. The frame is steel with a thick, upholstered filling. The legs are chromed steel. *Gijs Papvoine*

⬤⬤ **La Vendetta di Ulises** CD and DVD stand made of silver-colored metallic laminate, curved by two steel cables. It can be fixed to the wall and holds up to one hundred CDs and DVDs. *Luciano Bertoncini*

⬤⬤ **Finder** Horizontal or vertical magazine rack, in natural or white lacquered stainless steel. Because it is made of steel, the unit can be attached to the wall with a magnet. *Xavier Lust*

● ▪ **Planisfero** Lounge table with dual tempered glass tops. The upper piece of glass is movable. The supporting shafts are opaque chromed steel. *Arnaldo Gamba and Leila Guerra*

▪ ● **Basic** Container series in natural ash or maple, or lacquered in matte white. The back, separators, and interiors with drawers are in matte white, and the doors are in natural stainless steel. *Zed*

●● **Rolling** Chaise lounge made from one sheet of polished stainless steel, supported by a roller of the same material, covered with black rubber. The headrest and footrest are polyurethane. *Roberto Monte*

●● **Flex** Armchair with movable backrest. The frame is aluminum. *Stefan Heiliger*

**Unbroken Wave** These modular units have a polished stainless steel frame, covered with polyurethane and upholstered in black leather or orange elastic neoprene. The versatile pieces can be combined to form sofas, chairs, and ottomans. *Roberto Monte*

**Easy Stool** Stackable chair with chromed steel frame. The seat is natural birch and enamel. *Neunzig Design*

**Marcel** Stackable bed with chromed steel frame and sides in varnished wood.
*Hertel Klarhoefer*

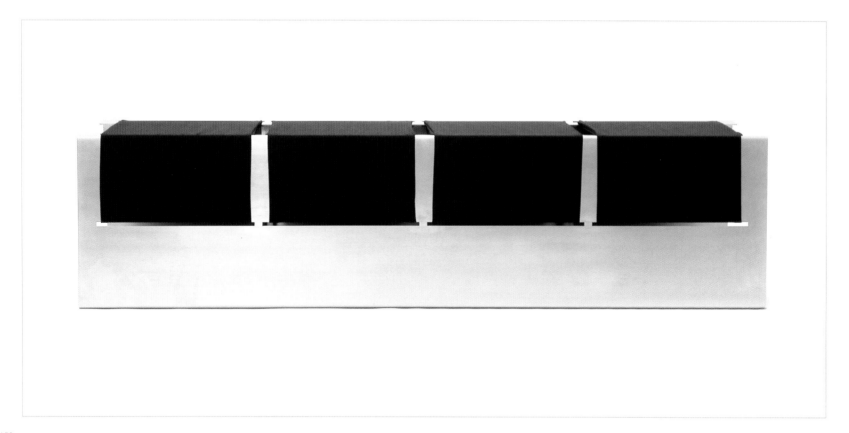

●● **Wait Room** Seating system for public spaces, with a chromed steel frame and
●● seat in taut fabric. *Roberto Monte*

●● **Ribbon** Small table supported by flat steel legs. The top is available in leather
●● or transparent or black glass. *PearsonLloyd*

**Tapis Roulant** Chaise lounge made of one sheet of polished stainless steel, wrapped in polyurethane cushions and covered in fabric. *Roberto Monte*

**Pascià** Night table made of stainless steel and wood. The door can be configured to open to the left or to the right. *Cantori*

**Hamaca** This hanging hammock is upholstered in leather and lightly cushioned. The hangers are chromed steel. *Patricia Urquiola*

**Alfombra Mota** Virgin wool carpet, with cotton on the reverse. Available in three sizes. *José A. Gandia*

DD 161

**Swoop Low/high** A small series of chairs with backrests and seats in molded cold foam, upholstered in fabric. The base is chromed metal. Also available on casters. *Ola Rune*

**Lima** Sofa and ottoman set with seams that accentuate the volumes of the backrest, seat, and armrests, giving it an air of harmony and calmness. *Gijs Papavoine*

●● **Metro** Chair with backrest and seat made of molded cold foam with Pullmaflex
●● support, upholstered in either fabric or leather. The legs are available in
chromed or silvered metal. *Thomas Sandell*

●□ **Mono** A series of chairs of varying heights. The seats and backrests are cold
●□ foam with Pullmaflex support, upholstered in fabric or leather. The legs come
in chromed or silvered steel. *Ola Rune*

●◦ **Retreat Funnel** Chair made of thin metal tubing; each tube is individually
◦◦ covered with angora yarn. *Louise Campbell*

◦● **Between** Series of chairs with metal frames, cut by laser, and seats covered
◦◦ in cork. *Louise Campbell*

◦◦ **Relief** Chaise lounge made from a single piece of slatted wood. The frame
◦● supports itself on the floor. *Louise Campbell*

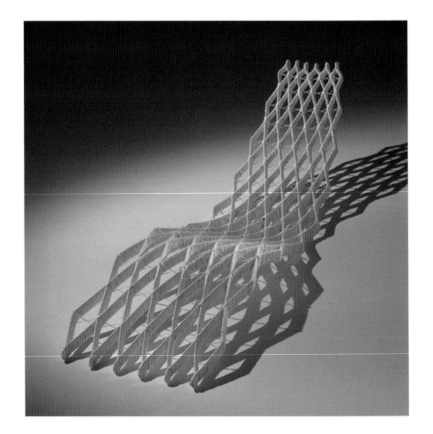

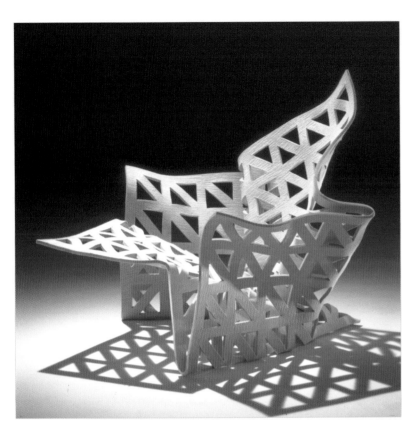

**Bless You** Chair made of wrinkled synthetic material and shaped strategically to strengthen the points at which it touches the floor. *Louise Campbell*

**Lotus** A surprisingly sturdy armchair made of slatted wood in the shape of a fruit bowl. *Louise Campbell*

**Honesty** Chair made of wooden slats. *Louise Campbell*

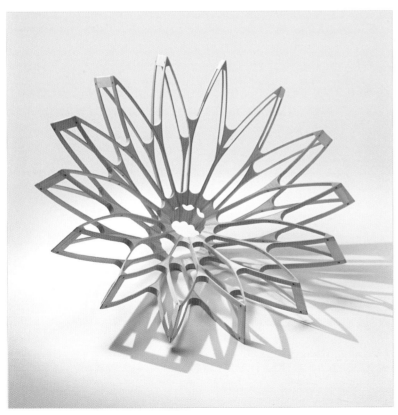

 **Together** Corner sofa with lines evocative of architectural design, rather than furniture design. The wooden frame is upholstered in leather. *EOOS*

**Soho** Round dining room table with space for four place settings. The base is enameled aluminum, and the top is transparent glass. *Silver Studio*

 **Look** An innovative sofa with a seat and backrest that fold to create more space. The wooden frame is completely upholstered in leather. *EOOS*

**Lucky Bergere** Ottoman and armchair with chromed stainless steel base. Available upholstered in fabric or soft, cushioned leather. *Emilio Nanni*

DD 168

**Targa** Extending dining room table with oak legs painted silver and a clear glass top. Also available with wengé legs. *Paolo Cattelan*

**Time** Extending dining room table with oak legs painted silver and a clear glass top. A strip of steel is inlaid in each of the legs. Also available with wengé legs. *Paolo Cattelan*

DD 169

**Foster** Corner sofa with upholstered steel frame and rectangular arm- and backrests. The minimalist legs are made of metal. *Norman Foster*

DD 170

**S 71F** Chair with wooden armrests, upholstered seat, and chromed steel legs. *Glen Oliver Löw*

**S 33** Chair with chromed steel frame. The seat and backrest are available upholstered in either leather or fabric. *Mart Stam*

**S 60** Armchair with chromed steel frame. The seat, armrests, and backrest are made of wood upholstered in rubber. *Glen Oliver Löw*

**S 70** Chair with curved steel tube frame. The seat and backrest are upholstered cold foam with removable covers. *Glen Oliver Löw*

**S 664** Chair with a steel frame, either chromed or varnished. The seat and backrest are made from a single sheet of wood. *Eddie Harlis*

●● **Jason Lite** Stackable chair with steel frame. The seat and backrest are leather-upholstered foam. *EOOS*

●● **Emma** Chair with chromed steel frame, upholstered in soft leather. *Studio Kronos*

●● **Argenta** Steel-framed chair with seat and backrest made of fiberglass. Available in a large number of standard colors, including light ivory, yellow, sulfur, burgundy, dark blue, turquoise, and anthracite gray, as well as custom colors. *Daifuku Design*

DD 174

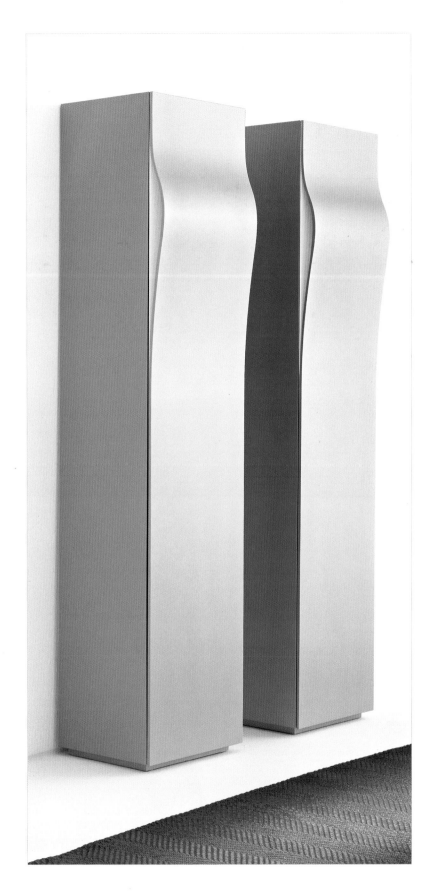

**Breeze** Containers for day or night, bathroom or bedroom, work or home. These units can stand horizontally or vertically, on the floor or hung on the wall. The horizontal model has a balanced door fitted with a cable-and-gas piston system. Available in matte white, matte aluminum, matte red, natural American walnut, or dark gray stained-oak finishes. Wooden or lacquered shelves and central drawers in the same finishes can be fitted into the interior. *Kazuhiro Yamanaka*

**Orgy** Sofa with laminated wood frame. The seat and backrest are cold foam upholstered in fabric, and the legs come in either chromed or silvered metal. An adjoining ottoman is also available. *Karim Rashid*

DD 178

**Boss** Stool with chromed steel base and seat upholstered in leather. The height is adjustable, and the leather is available in a variety of colors. *Gino Carollo*

**Super Natural** Chair with a polyamide shell, reinforced with fiberglass. *Ross Lovegrove*

**Zero** Armchair with wooden frame. The seat is rubber foam, and the base is available in either silvered or chrome-lacquered metal. *Marre Moerel*

 **Uptown** Sofa with wooden frame. The base, backrest, and seat are nonflammable cold foam upholstered in fabric or leather. The legs are available in either chromed or silvered metal. *Eero Koivisto*

**Giada** Chair with chromed steel frame. The seat and backrest are upholstered in cushioned, soft leather or fabric. *David Obendorfer*

**Du** Chair with chromed metal frame and cushioned seat upholstered in fabric. *Gastone Rinaldi*

DD 182

 **Toto** Swivel stool with chromed steel leg. The height is adjustable, and the seat is available in either leather or wood. *Paolo Cattelan*

 **Cosy** Cube-shaped seat made of polyester, varnished in a variety of colors. *Studio Vertijet*

●● **Mónaco** Dining room table with wengé legs that rest on a chromed steel base. The table top can be wengé or transparent glass. *Giorgio Cattelan*

●● **Harry** Dining room table and chair set with chromed steel frame. The top is white melamine, as are the seats and backrests of the chairs. *Hertel Klarhoefer*

**Citizen** Prism-shaped sofa with sharp lines reminiscent of cut glass. Made from polyurethane foam over a steel frame, upholstered in polyester. *Alfredo Häberli*

**Violet** Armchair with chromed or painted steel frame. The seat and backrest are upholstered partially in leather. Also available completely upholstered in either leather or fabric. *Giancarlo Vegni*

●● **Couture** This series of chairs uses traditionally printed fabrics, as well as digitally printed fabrics, embroidery, leather, and laser-cut fabrics. *Tord Boontje*

●● **Max Max** Armchair and ottoman made of cold foam with permanent and removable fabric covers. The base is stainless steel. *Zed*

**Trace** This stackable chair can be used outdoors as well as indoors. *Shin Azumi*

**Corso** High chair with steel frame entirely covered in foam and upholstered in leather. *Paolo Piva*

●● **Woody** The chairs in this collection are made entirely of ash and can be
equipped with metal armrests covered in leather or with a cushioned seat.
*Daifuku Design*

●● **Tavolo** Minimalist table with innovative twisted legs made of chromed steel. The top is wood. *Paolo Piva*

●● **Smock** Swivel chair with steel frame and seat covered in nonflammable polyurethane foam. The leather upholstery is removable, and the base is stainless steel. *Patricia Urquiola*

●● **Rodeo Drive** Extendable dining room table with polished stainless steel base and a top made of transparent and opaque glass. *Giorgio Cattelan*

●● **Nude Dimensions** Chaise lounge made of birch and covered with a layer of padded foam. *Burovormkrijgers*

DD 191

●● **Marinella** Chaise lounge with wooden frame, filled with foam and upholstered in leather. *Giovanni Casellato*

**⋮⋮ 4 to 8** This table can convert from four to eight place settings, thanks to the removable external ring. The base and leg are both stainless steel. The ring and fixed top are available in opaque lacquers of different colors. *Arik Levy*

**Easy** Armchair with wooden frame padded and upholstered in wool. *Jan Melis*

**Transform** One-seater armchair with wooden frame in ash, covered with polyurethane and upholstered in fabric. The backrest has two positions. *For Use*

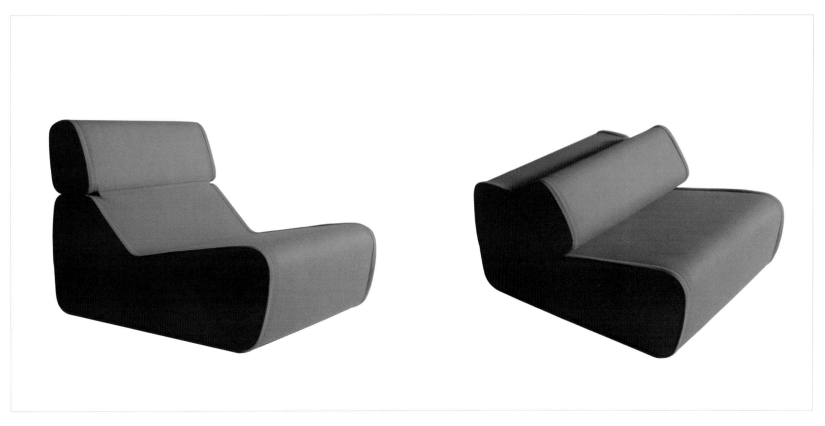

**::** **Sira** Table with frame in calibrated steel, lacquered in textured aluminum. A magazine rack is set in the oak top, which is available in a natural bleached finish, wengé, or cherry lacquered white or orange. An auxiliary tray and casters are also available. *Héctor Diego*

DD 194

**Marais Bed** This bed, like the other pieces in the series, is characterized by its pyramid profile. The base is finished in brilliant aluminum, and the fabric or leather coverings are completely removable. *Paola Navone*

**Tatanka** Folding table with metal frame in brushed nickel, finished with transparent paint. The top is ash stained in a mocha color. *Grafite Design*

**Logica** Minimalist chair, available in several colors. *Daniele Lago*

DD 197

:: **Clip** Padded double bed with a folded frame reminiscent of a paperclip. The headboard can bend. The coverings are completely removable. A side table with a lacquered frame and a thin glass top completes the picture. *Patricia Urquiola*

:: **Marais** Sofa characterized by its pyramid profile. The base is finished in brilliant aluminum; the removable coverings are available in fabric or leather.
*Paola Navone*

**Rondó** Dining room table with chromed stainless steel base and top in either glass or marble. *Giorgio Cattelan*

**Capellini** Dining room table with steel tube frame, lacquered white. The smoked glass top is supported by the ring of the base. *Patrick Norguet*

**H2O** Dining room table held up by a single piece of chromed stainless steel tube, sculpted into a three-point support. The top is transparent glass. *Massimo Iosa Ghini*

**Oval** Table with iron frame and glass top, onto which leaves and flowers have been printed in white. The legs are iron varnished in black. *Tord Boontje*

DD 201

# lights

Just as furniture contributes to the sense of an architectural space, light, whether natural or artificial, and by either its presence or absence, serves to model these spaces. To find a comfortable balance, it is essential to complement natural light with sources of artificial light, according to the requirements of each place.

In the nineteenth century, the discovery of electricity led to the appearance of the first incandescent lamps. Ever since, the evolution of the form has encompassed different types of lights and lamps: the conventional incandescent lights, plus halogens and fluorescents. We have seen the implementation of ceiling lights, footlights, table lights, and exterior lights. But far beyond the latest function of lamps stands their amazing integration into the spaces of humanity. These pieces create a sense of the triumph that the technology was meant to realize. In this chapter, one is given a generous appreciation of the proposals made by well-recognized designers, and points pertaining to the design of illumination itself.

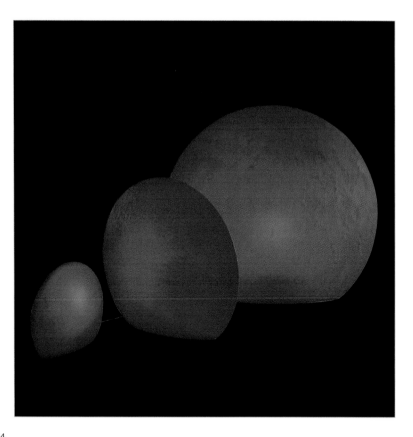

- ● ● **Eggo** Indoor/outdoor lamp made of polyethylene, in assorted matte colors. *Monica Lipken*

- ● ● **Gap** Table lamp with base and shade in silk over a metal frame. The electrical cable is transparent. *Alexander Seifried*

- ● ● **Otto** Lamp that doubles as a stool for indoor and outdoor use. The seat cushion is fabric-upholstered foam, and the lampshade is polyethylene finished in various matte colors. *Georg Draser*

◐ **Light Up 1** Wall lamp with a rectangular acrylic glass shade over a fluorescent bulb. The shade is available in several matte colors. *Olaf Kitzig*

◑ **Light Up 3** Square wall lamp with an acrylic glass shade over a fluorescent bulb. The shade is available in several matte colors. *Olaf Kitzig*

**Kind of Magic** Lamp with aluminum base and polypropylene shade. Floor and table models are both available. The power supply, switch, plug, and main support are all transparent. *Black & Blum*

**Stand Up** Polypropylene lamp available in matte white. The bulb is in the base, which gives the piece a very distinctive look. *Hopf and Wortmann*

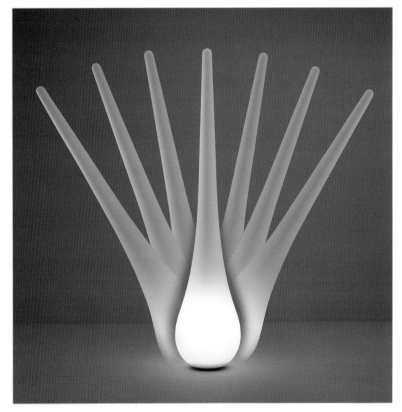

●● **Mellanstrut** Ceiling lamp made from nonflammable material and available
○○ in matte white. A cylindrical form is suspended from a square panel. *Annika
Grottell*

●○ **Viper** Wall or ceiling lamp with a flexible arm, allowing the lamp to be adapt-
○○ ed to a variety of uses. *Daifuku Design*

●● **Strale** Directional hanging lamp that uses a halogen projector bulb with a
○● parabolic reflector. *Album*

**Pure Glass** The glass shades on these hanging lamps are part of a series of versatile glass objects. Each shade has a piece of synthetic material, available in several colors, around its center. *Vogt and Weizenegger*

**Waki** Ceiling lamp with a blown opal glass body and a chromed cast aluminum base. The lamp comes in two sizes; the smaller version can be mounted as track lighting and used vertically or horizontally. *Daifuku Design*

DD 210

**Reading** Table lamp, shaped like a seated man reading, sculpted from chromed zinc. The bulb socket and power supply are transparent, and the book-shaped shade is blue semi-translucent propylene. *Black & Blum*

**Climbing** Wall lamp, shaped like a climbing man, sculpted from chromed zinc. It attaches to the wall with a single screw. The bulb socket and power supply are transparent. *Black & Blum*

**Libellule** Hanging lamp in the shape of a dragonfly, sculpted from chromed zinc. The bulb socket and power supply are transparent, and the wings of the dragonfly are translucent propylene. *Black & Blum*

**Little Devil** Table lamp with a red polypropylene shade that projects the silhouette of an angel. The bulb socket, power supply, and plug are black. *Black & Blum*

**Cloud 9** Hanging lamp with shade constructed from colored polypropylene. A translucent cord suspends the lamp from the ceiling. *Black & Blum*

**Seed** Hanging lamp with flat polypropylene shade. The shade acts as a projector, diffusing light from a central slit. *Black & Blum*

**Liquid Light** Ceiling and floor lamps in the form of water droplets. The shade is made of white polypropylene. *Büro Für Form*

**Liquid Light** Floor and table lamps in the form of water droplets. The shade is made of white polypropylene, and the lamps can be used indoors or outdoors. *Büro Für Form*

**Cross Light** Hanging lamp with polyethylene shade. *Jan Melis*

**Ilde T2** Table lamp with metallic base and shade that diffuses light. Available with an attached dimmer. *David Abad*

**Josephine** Standing lamp made of sheets of acrylic glass. A fluorescent tube runs from the base to the top of the lamp, giving off a soft glow through the glass body. *Burovormkrijgers*

**Flap Flap** Table or floor lamp with white polypropylene shade and colored polyethylene base. *Büro Für Form*

●● **Trilight** Hanging or table lamp with a stainless steel shade divided into three leaves. The shade is available in several colors. *Burovormkrijgers*

●● **DL 800** Standing outdoor lamp made of stainless steel. The shade is steel and plastic; the height of the arm on which the shade sits is adjustable. *Siteco*

**Futurel** Standing lamps available in two versions, one of which has an adjustable arm. The lamp support is made of polished steel, and the plastic shade is available in several different colors. *Siteco*

**Amelie** Table lamp with metal body painted in an aluminum color. The oval-shaped glass shade is available in satin or transparent blue, brown, red, or bottle green. *Harry & Camila*

**Hexal** Hanging panel lamp with aluminum body. *Siteco*

DD 219

**Vistosa** Stainless steel gooseneck lamp, designed for use on tables. *Siteco*

 **Bruco** Wall lamp with nickel-plated metal base and blown glass shade in matte white. *Vico Magistretti*

**Max** Wall lamp with aluminum, glass fiber, and stainless steel body. The switch is integrated into the base, which also houses the transformer. The shade can rotate 180°. *Ingo Maurer*

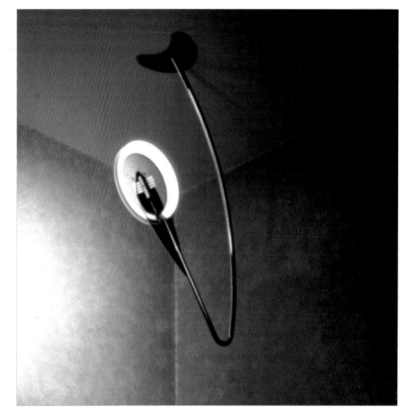

 **Nast** Ceiling lamp with a ring-shaped fluorescent tube covered by a hanging shade of 7,500 Swarovski crystals. *Fuseproject*

**Occhio Faro** Versatile lamp with a curved metal body and a halogen projector bulb that emits light from the sides. This piece can be mounted on the wall, the ceiling, or even a table. *Massimo Iosa Ghini*

**Lampscapes** Hanging lamps available in groups of three, with synthetic shades of varying sizes. The profiles of the shades give the impression of a landscape. *Studio Frederik Roijé*

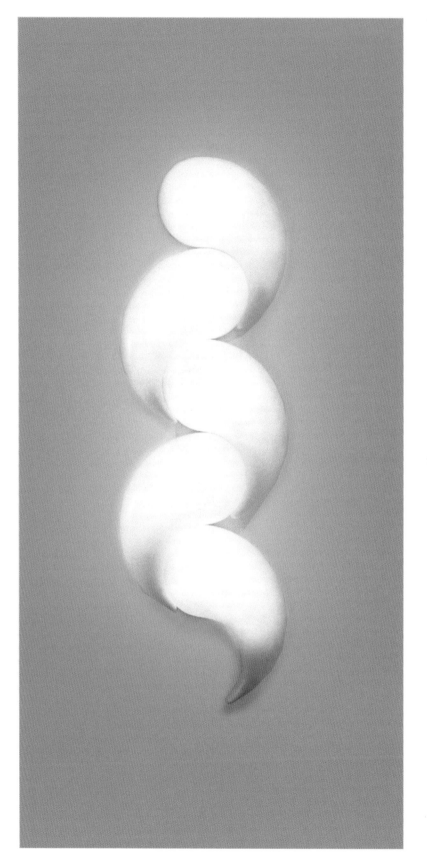

**Chakra** Wall lamp with handmade fiberglass shade. *Guglielmo Berchicci*

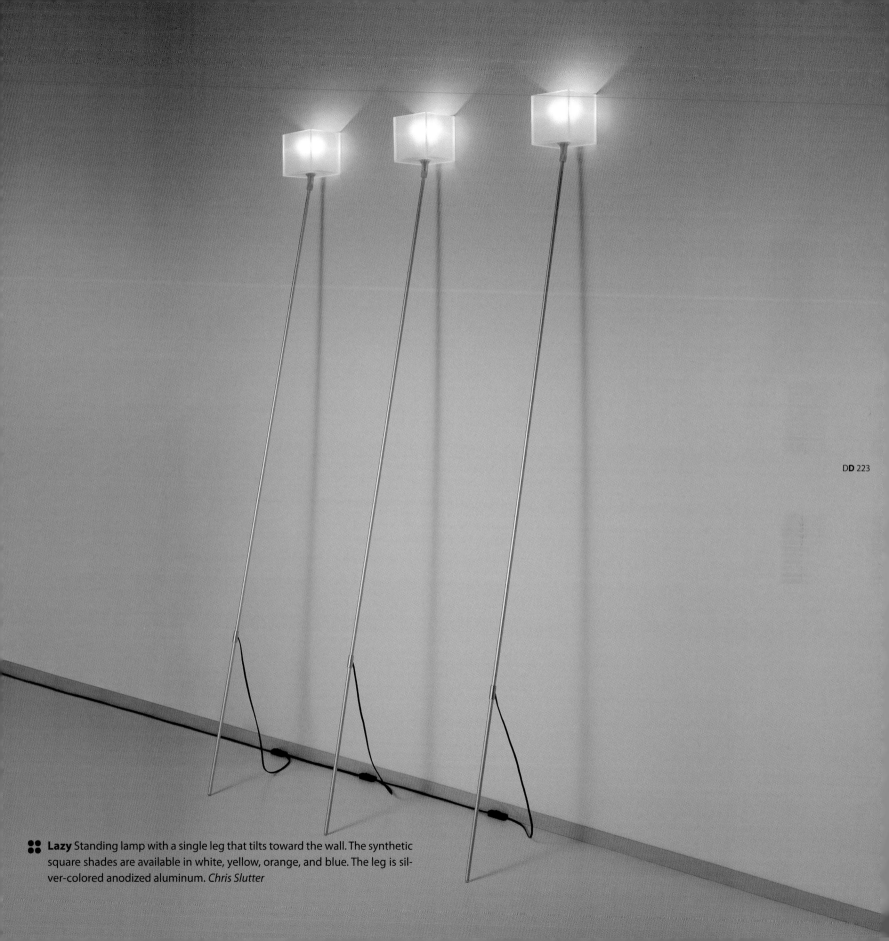

**Lazy** Standing lamp with a single leg that tilts toward the wall. The synthetic square shades are available in white, yellow, orange, and blue. The leg is silver-colored anodized aluminum. *Chris Slutter*

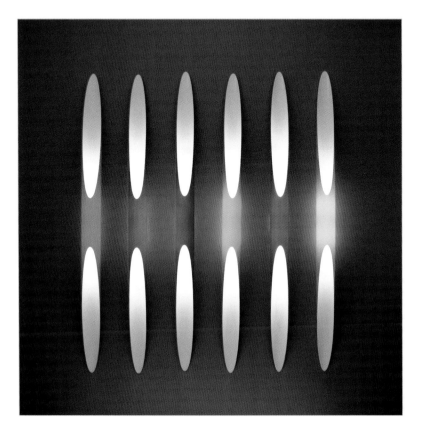

**Shakti** Standing or wall lamp with a colored Plexiglas shade. The shade lets light through openings at the top and bottom. *Marzio Rusconi Clerici*

⠿ **Bulb and Candle** Table lamp made of a single piece of acrylic glass with a bulb in the base. The lamp is available in several colors. *Gilles Roudot*

DD 225

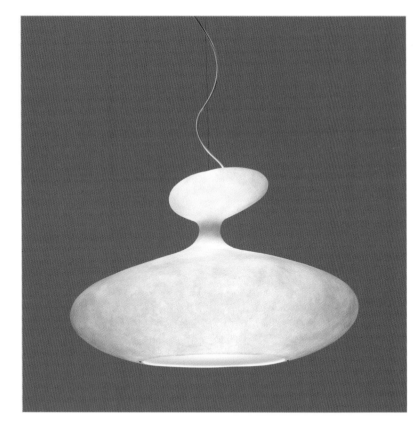

**E.T.A. and E.T.A. Baby** Standing lamp with a one-piece shade handmade from ecological fiberglass, supported by a metal frame. *Guglielmo Berchicci*

**E.T.A. Sat** Hanging lamp with a handmade fiberglass shade over a metal frame. *Guglielmo Berchicci*

**Atollo** Hanging lamp with blown glass shade available in transparent amber or eggshell colors. The body is metal varnished gray. *Carlo Nason*

**Noglobe** Hanging and table lamps with white spherical polyethylene shades. The table version has a transparent acrylic glass base. *Laura Agnoletto and Marzio Rusconi Clerici*

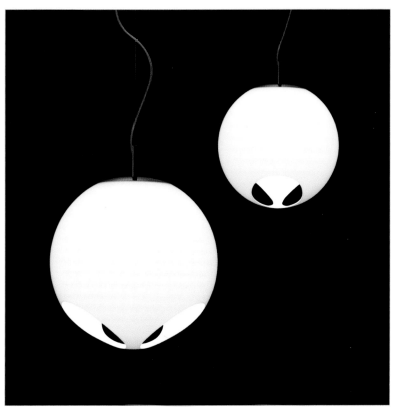

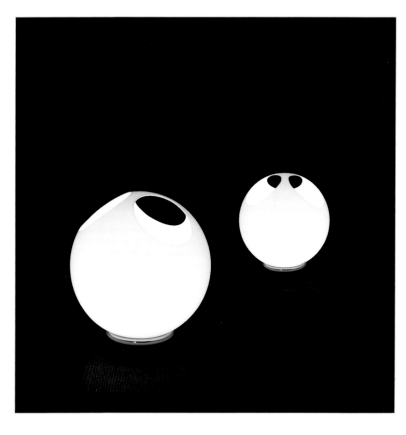

DD 228

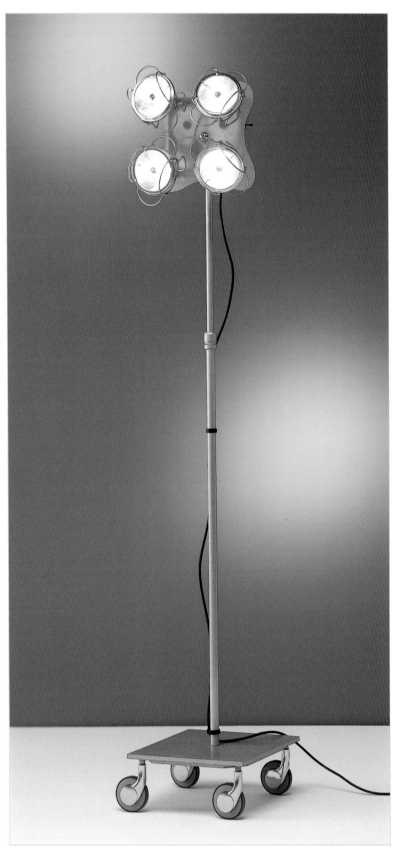

**Strale** Standing and wall lamps that use halogen projector bulbs with parabolic reflectors. Each of the four bulbs can be angled separately. The body is aluminum, and the height can be adjusted. *Album*

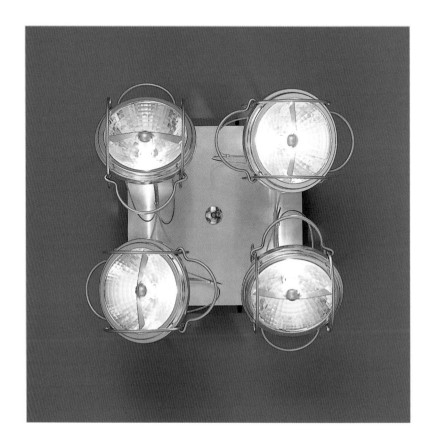

**Fortuny** Standing lamp with a steel tube body. The cotton shade is available in black or beige, and the inside of the shade is white. The body is varnished with black or titanium epoxy powder. The lamp can be tilted, raised, and lowered. *Mariano Fortuny and Madrazo*

DD 229

**Babe** Wall or table lamp with aluminum and stainless steel base. The shade can rotate 360°. *Nils Jann*

**Solar II** A series of hanging lamps with extruded aluminum shades that can be tilted at any angle. *Massimo Iosa Ghini*

●● **Toric** Hanging lamp with body and shade in painted metal. *Patrick Norguet*

●● **Luup Poller** Standing lamp with a metallic body. The lamp uses spotlight bulbs. *On Design*

**Yu** Series of wall, table, and ceiling lamps, available with either one or two blown glass shades. *Marzio Rusconi Clerici*

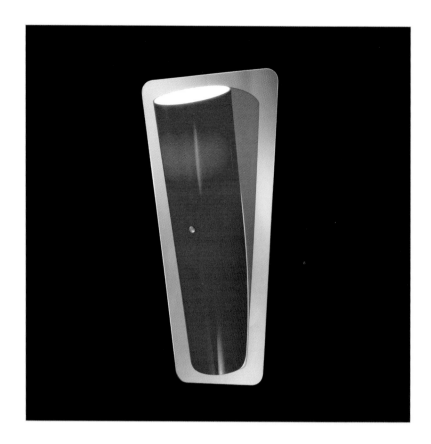

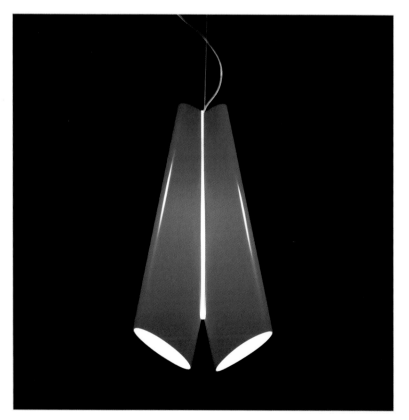

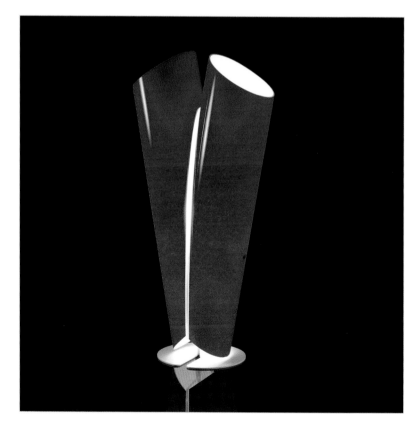

**Rainy Day** Circular lamp with an extra-long power supply for easy rearranging. Several units can be stacked to make a standing lamp for the floor or table, or a single lamp can be mounted on the wall. The molded polyethylene body is available in translucent white or acid yellow. *Kazuhiro Yamanaka*

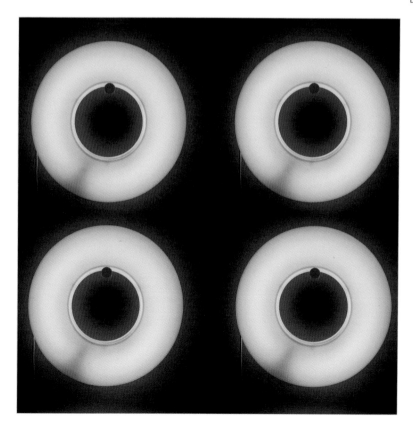

**Serena** Hanging lamp with chromed steel base and body. The shade is brushed aluminum. *Josep Patsí*

**Annton and Ann** Wall lamps with rectangular and cube-shaped transparent glass bodies and metal fittings. Both versions use powerful halogen bulbs that can be rotated 360°. *Jonas Kressel and Ivo Schelle*

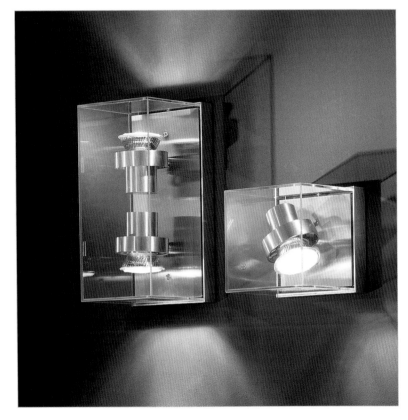

**Lumiera** Hanging lamp with hand-blown molded borosilicate glass shade. The dichroic bulbs give off direct and indirect light. *Album*

**Medusina** Hanging lamp with hand-blown molded borosilicate glass shade with a partially frosted finish. *Album*

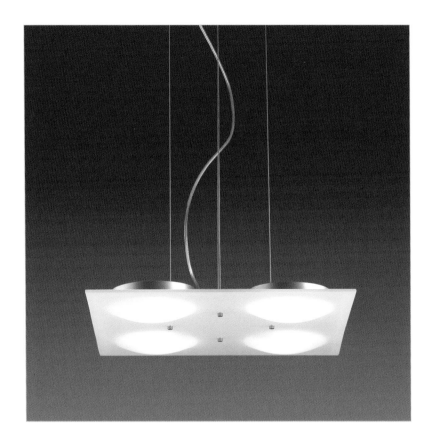

**Lario** Hanging lamp with base from which thin cables support both sides of the bulbs in an elongated circular form. The bulbs are set at different heights.
*Piero Lissoni*

**Duna** Hanging lamp with matte aluminum body and opaque glass shade.
*Alex Sánchez*

DD 237

**TMC** Series of standing lamps with chromed metal bodies and cross-shaped bases. The shades are white Perspex, and the height of the lamp can be adjusted. *Miguel Mila*

⣿ **Vague Stelle** Hanging lamp with a medieval feel, originally designed for a restaurant. *Antoni de Moragas*

⣿ **Verformlampe** Hanging lamp with thick molded porcelain shades. Also available in a table model. *Sandra Lindner*

● ● **X Wing** Hanging lamp with a metal body varnished in aluminum. The bulb is
surrounded by a Pyrex glass shade and fitted with a transparent acrylic glass
shade available in gray, orange, and yellow. *Marc Krusin*

● ● **Ierace** Hanging lamp with aluminum body. The fluorescent bulb is fitted with
a transparent blown glass shade. *Matali Crasset*

DD 240

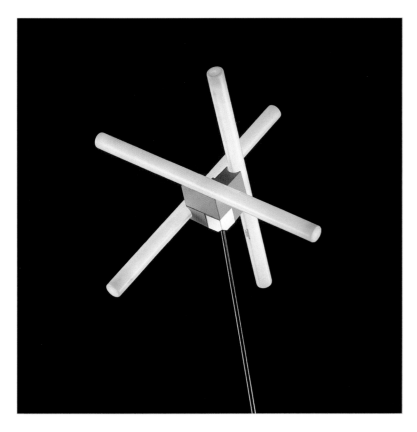

**Bib Luz** Lamp designed to be attached to a bookcase. A metal arm extends from the book-shaped steel base. The lamp uses a halogen bulb. *Oscar Tusquets*

**Olvidad** Standing lamp with three crossed fluorescent bulbs on an aluminum body. *Pepe Cortés*

**L'arbre à reflets** Lamp with metal support painted silver. The shade is made of mirrors painted with acrylic. *Matali Crasset*

**Light Up** Lamp with metal body painted in a silver color. The plastic shade is painted with acrylic. *Matali Crasset*

**Tonic** Table lamp consisting of a halogen bulb suspended inside a hand-blown borosilicate glass container. The container can be filled with clear or colored liquids, and the bulb can be removed from the container. *Album*

**LP Radiator** Hanging lamp with steel body. The fluorescent bulb is fitted with a shade made of acrylic glass sheets inlaid with pieces of silk. *Louise Campbell*

**Placid** Rabbit-shaped table lamp with halogen bulb and soft resin body. The on/off mechanism is a pressure sensor located in the ears. *Album*

**Ais** Table lamp with a thin crystal shade in the shape of a drinking glass. The shade is covered in small pieces of colored crystallized plastic. *Takahide Sano*

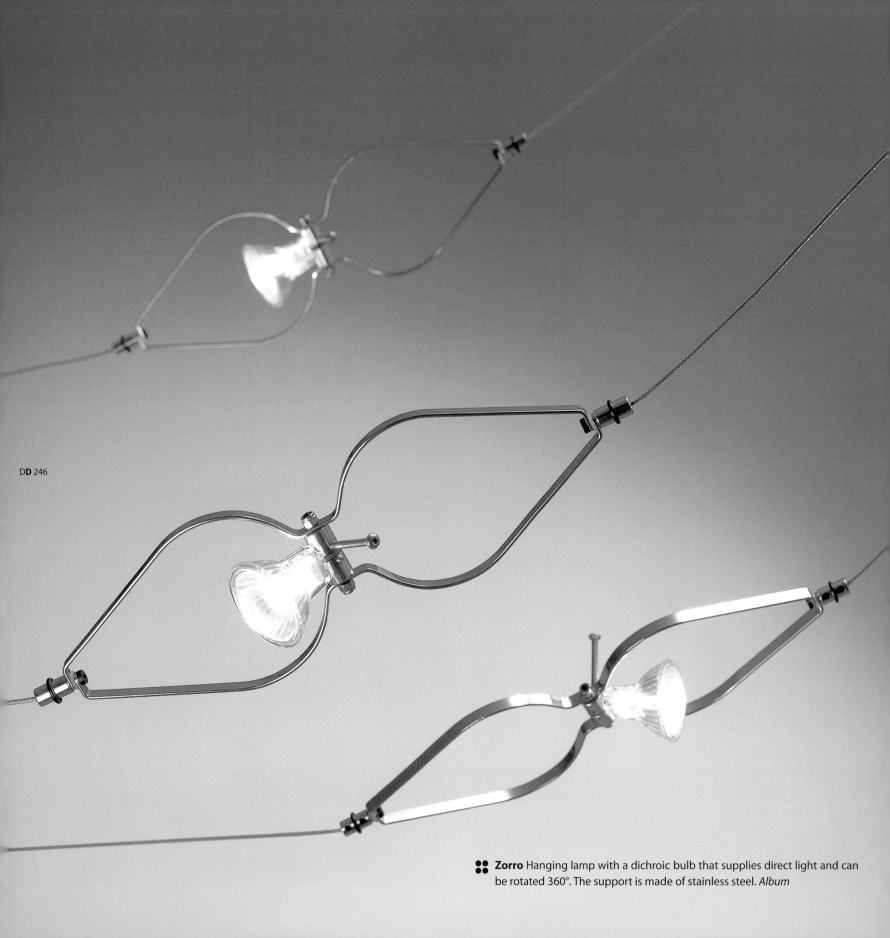

DD 246

**∷ Zorro** Hanging lamp with a dichroic bulb that supplies direct light and can be rotated 360°. The support is made of stainless steel. *Album*

**Ray Bow** Standing lamp with either three or five chromed metal tubes terminating in bulbs. The arms can be moved to direct light. *Gregorio Spini*

**Toma** This sculptural table lamp is made of steel and aluminum. *Elmar Thome*

**Lila** Standing lamp with chromed steel base and transparent or black Plexiglas shade. *Gregorio Spini*

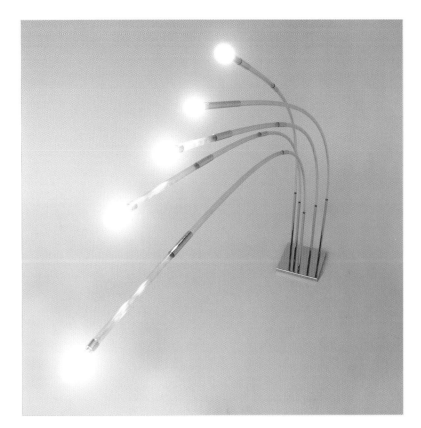

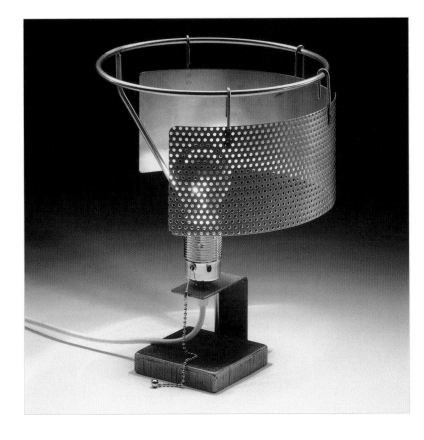

DD 248

●● **Rondine** Hanging lamp with a dichroic bulb and a molded glass shade. The
●● surface of the shade is silk-screened. *Album*

●● **Boogie Woogie** Table lamp with a stainless steel and anodized aluminum
●● body. The shade comes in colored or white silk and is finished with tape.
*Paul Imbrechts*

●● **Console** Table lamp with polished cast-bronze body. The shade is opaque
●● Murano glass. *Gerrit Holdijk*

**Asia** Table lamp with matte or polished brass body. The shade is black silk. *Fitz Licht*

**Gem** Hanging lamp made of two polycarbonate hemispheres, which have been photoengraved. The two halves are held together by the cables that secure the fixture to the ceiling. *Paul Andreu*

**Lp** Table lamp made of two pieces of hand-forged aluminum. *Jan Melis*

 **Drawn to the Light** Hanging lamp composed of thirty-six pieces of porcelain that seem to float around the bulb. The base is also porcelain. *Scabetti*

**Pendant** Hanging lamp with a polished aluminum inner shade and a transparent and opaque glass outer shade. *Louise Campbell*

**Fold** Hanging lamp with chromed or painted metal body. The opaque white glass shade is enclosed in a screen of transparent blown glass. *Theo Williams*

**Tulip** Standing lamp with stainless steel and nickel body. The five pieces of the shade, made of silk on an aluminum frame, unzip open and zip closed like petals. *Quasar*

**Scuffia** Hanging lamp with painted steel body. The cone-shaped lampshade is made from a composite material. *Album*

●● **EfQus** Hanging lamp with stainless steel and aluminum body. The shade is
○○ white cotton. *Jan des Bouvrie*

●○ **On/Off** Standing lamp with stainless steel and aluminum body. The base
○● houses an on/off mechanism controlled by the angle of the main support.
The shade is white cotton. *Peter Mac Cann*

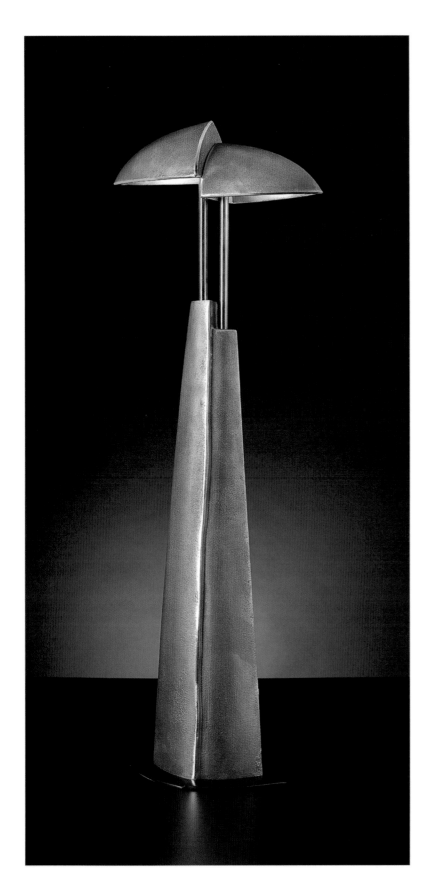

● ● **Ara** Table lamp made of polished aluminum and bronze. *Quasar*
● ●

● ● **Mujay** Table lamp made of semitransparent blue Murano glass. *Edward*
● ● *van Vliet*

D**D** 254

**Pan Am** Series of hanging, standing, wall, or ceiling lamps with polished aluminum shades that rotate 360° and swivel 270° on an axle. The lamps use halogen bulbs. *Büro Für Form*

**Oby** Series of hanging and table lamps. The shade is white porcelain. In the table model, the shade is set on an aluminum bar, and the height can be adjusted. *Büro Für Form*

**Jetsa** Table lamp with glass shade. The outside of the shade is eggshell white, while the inside is matte white. *Victoria*

**Paralume** Table lamp with metal body lacquered with white epoxy powder. The shade is eggshell white Murano glass. *Ufficio Stile Murano Due*

**WK 919** Table lamp with brushed steel body and shade in two pieces of light blue or white glass. The shade can be square or round. *Heinz Klein and Georg Leidig*

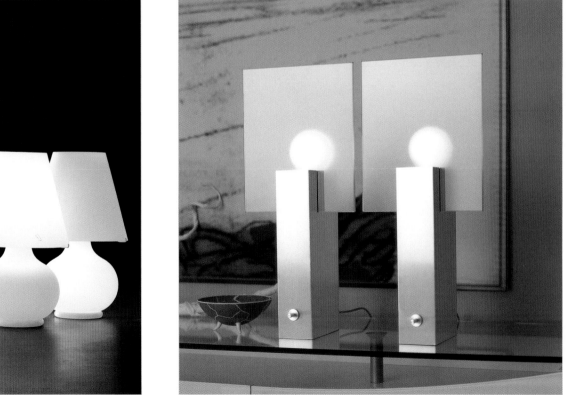

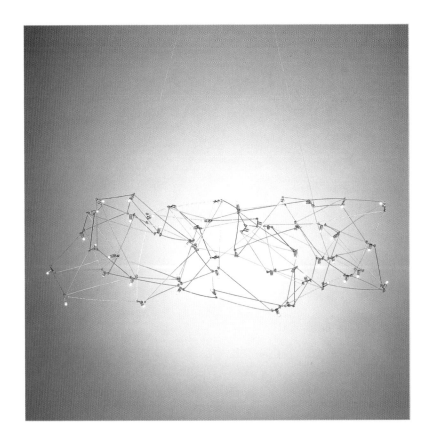

**Universe** Hanging lamp made of nickel filaments. *Jan Pauwels*

**Vase** Table lamp with dichroic halogen bulb. The shade is transparent glass, with a divider between the bulb compartment and the vase. *Victoria*

●● **WK 913 Casino** Table lamp with marble base and nickel- or gold-plated body. The shade is rectangular soft polyester. *Heinz Klein and Georg Leidig*

●● **Pacu** Standing lamps with rounded metallic bodies. This lamp comes in two sizes. *On Design*

**Tube** Standing lamp with a tube-shaped shade made of acrylic glass housing a fluorescent bulb. The base is painted titanium metal. *Christian Deuber*

**QWF** Wall lamp with aluminum body varnished in matte silver. *Industria 191*

**QTW** Wall lamp with aluminum body varnished in matte silver. The power supply is transparent. *Industria 191*

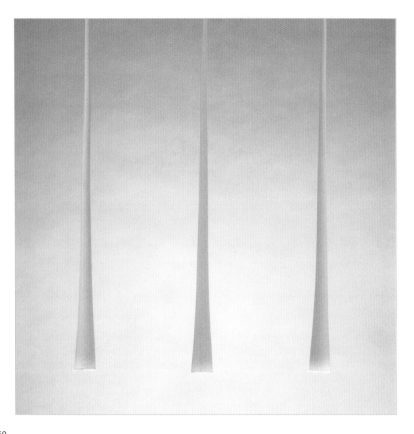

**The Line** Hanging lamp made of silicone with particles of white metal powder. *Marco Schregardus*

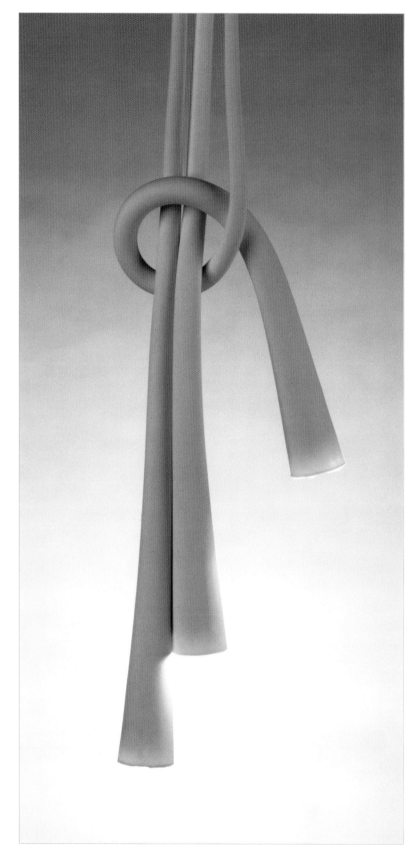

 **Omega** Table lamp with chromed and anodized aluminum body. The hinge uses magnets, making the lamp fully adjustable. *Jos Muller*

**Compass** Hanging lamp in aluminum. *Jos Muller*

**Portofino** Hanging lamp with aluminum body and transparent blue glass shade. *Jan des Bouvrie*

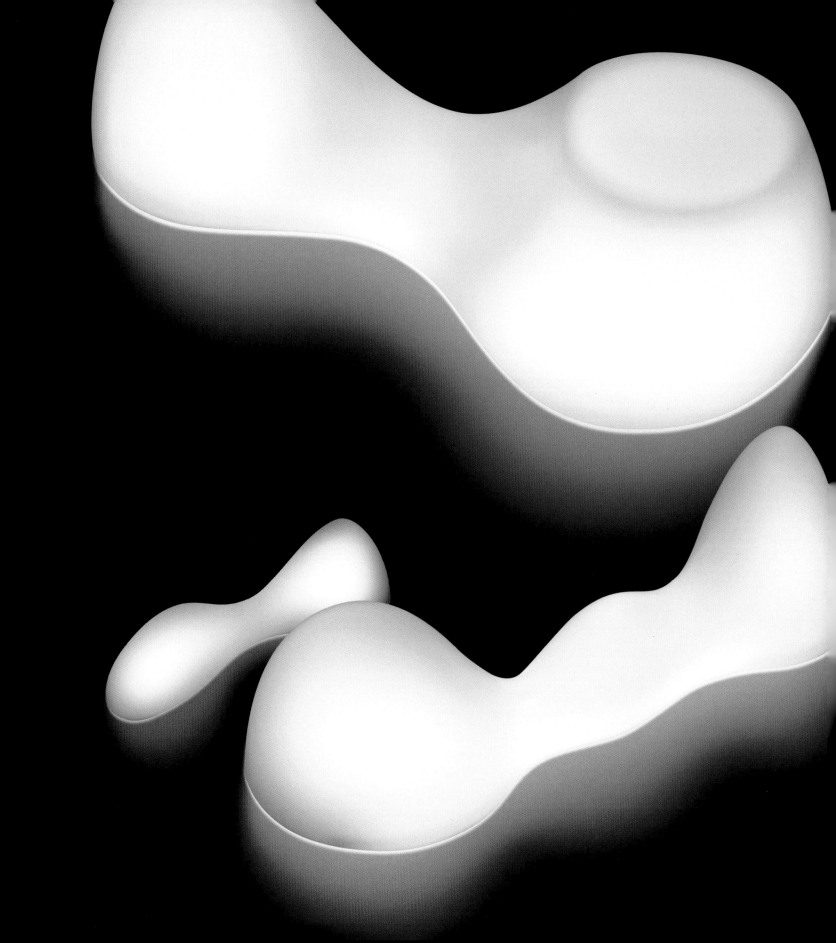

DD 262

⠿ **Blob** Standing lamp with shade and body made of white molded polypropylene. Available in three sizes, for indoor and outdoor use. *Karim Rashid*

**Orbit** Series of table lamps with colored polypropylene and chromed metal bodies. The lamp comes in three sizes and is available in red, blue, white, translucent yellow, orange, burgundy, and magenta. *Hiroshi Tsunoda*

●● **Himiko** Named for the first Japanese empress, this ceiling lamp is characterized by its pointed silhouette and rounded layers. The folded panels of the shade are made of polypropylene. The lamp comes in red, blue, white, translucent yellow, orange, burgundy, and magenta. *Hiroshi Tsunoda*

●● **P.P. Emotions** This table lamp has a jellyfish-shaped transparent polypropylene shade. Each set of six comes with an assortment of colored panels, which can be switched and replaced to change the lamp's color. *Hiroshi Tsunoda*

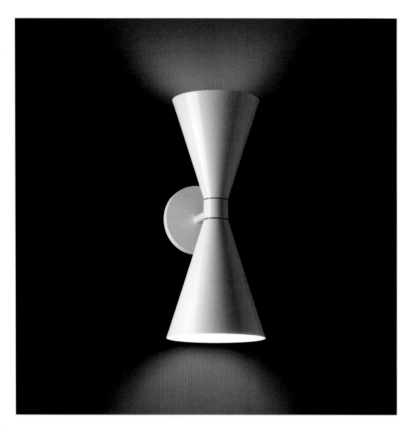

DD 266

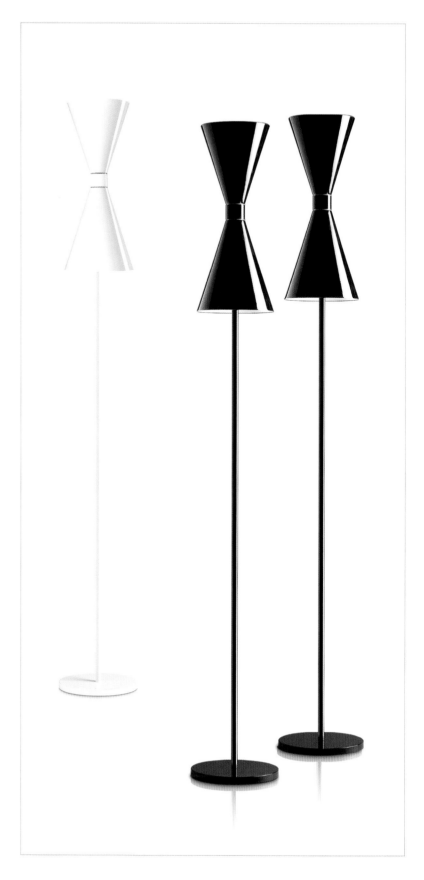

**⣿ Diabolo** Series of standing or wall lamps available with either one or two shades that can be oriented up or down. The body of the lamp is metal lacquered in black or white. *Enric Gregorio*

 **Zia** Table lamp with shade in white frosted Murano glass. The base is nickel. *Oriano Favaretto*

 **Cino** Table lamp with shade in white frosted Murano glass. The base is in metal lacquered opaque white. *Lorenzo Damiani*

 **Atmosfera** Table lamp with shade in white frosted Murano glass. The base is in chromed metal. *Giovanni D´Ambrosio*

DD 268

●● **Sino** Flexible hanging lamp with aluminum shade. The angular form allows
●● light to be accurately directed. *Belux*

●● **Select** Standing lamp with two rotating heads, each equipped with reflec-
●● tors and antiglare grills. *Belux*

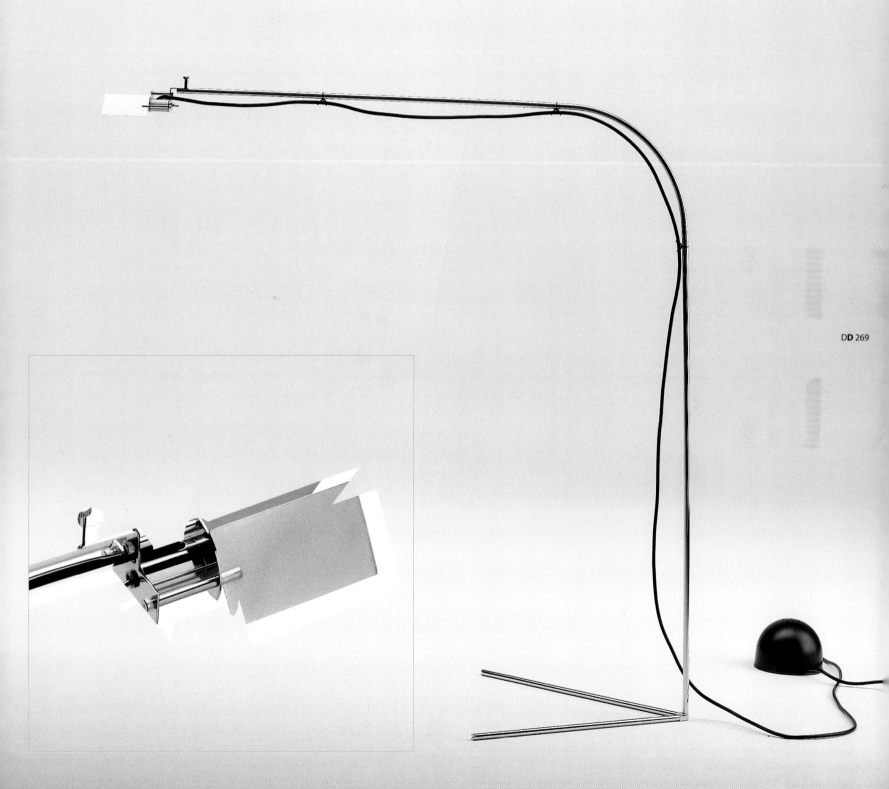

**Flamingo** Standing lamp with shaped chromed-iron body. The frame can be dismantled. The matte anodized aluminum shade has fins for directing light. The switch is built into the shade. *Álvaro Siza Vieira*

DD 269

**Carvallo** Table lamp with polished brass, matte brass, and matte nickel body. The shade is available in several light tones of silk. *Fitz Licht*

**Siena** Table lamp with polished or matte brass body. The shade is available in silk or in gold- or silver-brushed lacquer. *Fitz Licht*

**Grazia** Table lamp with polished brass body and gray silk shade. *Fitz Licht*

● ● **Joint Terra** Standing lamp with brushed steel body and six lights in blown
● ○ glass shades. The shades come in brilliant white, blue, or amber finishes.
*Mauro Marzollo*

● ● **Contessina** Hanging lamp with metal body in lacquered aluminum. The
● ● shade is available in amber, white, blue, or black frosted Murano glass. *Carlo
Nason*

Class 40/60

DD 272

**Class 40/60** Hanging lamp sets in two sizes. These lights can be mounted on a track in sets of two to five lamps. *Ufficio Stile I Tre*

🞄🞄 **Finn** Table and standing lamps with two shades, the outer in transparent Murano glass and the inner in white frosted Murano glass. The base is chromed metal or metal lacquer in matte aluminum with chromed details. *Takahide Sano*

**Lantern** Round table lamp with aluminum body and cotton shade. *Marc Krusin*

**Pacchet** Wall lamp with matte white varnished metal. The acrylic glass shade is available in white, red, or blue. *Charles Williams*

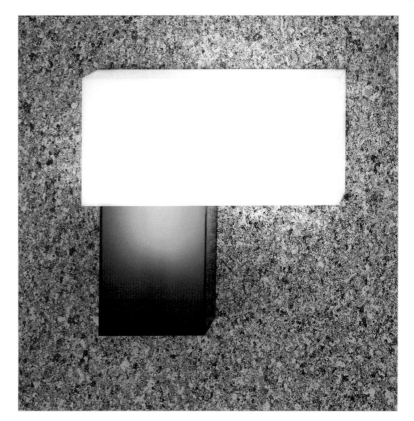

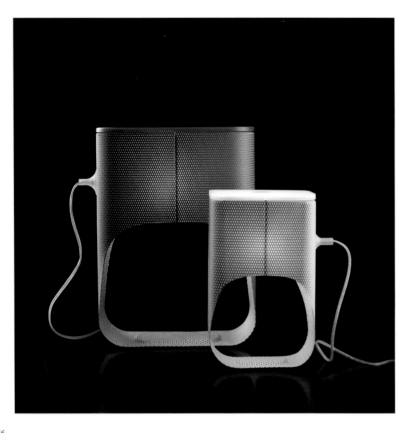

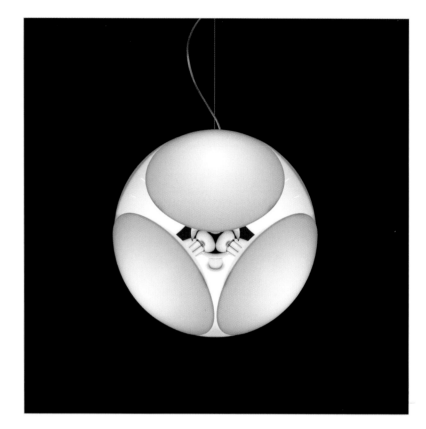

●○ **Bague** Table lamp available in three sizes. The body is a perforated metal net
○○ coated in silicone resin, and the shade is satin. *Patricia Urquiola and Eliana
Gerotto*

○● **Bubble** Hanging lamp with chromed metal body and polished polycarbonate
○○ shade. Emits 360° of light from the spherical shade. *Valerio Bottin*

●● **Thor** Standing lamp made of layers of lacquered aluminum to project multi-
●● directional light. The shade on the upper part directs light upward and down-
ward. *Luca Nichetto and Gianpietro Gai*

**Love** Standing lamp with internal light that consists of two aluminum rings surrounding an electromagnetic film in the center. *Fuseproject*

DD 277

●● **Bulb 3** Hanging lamp with yellow copper or nickel body. The three bulbs are
○○ bare. *Quasar*

●● **Lulu** Hanging lamp available in two sizes. The body is finished in nickel, and
○○ the shade is transparent blown glass with embedded crystal pearls. *Ufficio
Stile Aureliano Toso*

**Marilyn** Standing lamp with brilliant white Murano glass shade, available with either a blue-and-white frosted or black spiral. The base is tapering metal lacquered silver. *Carlo Nason*

**Primavera** Table lamp with polished brass body and light-colored silk shade. *Fitz Licht*

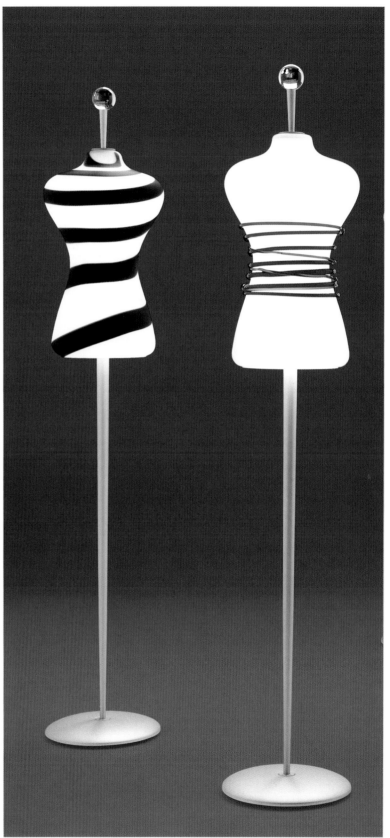

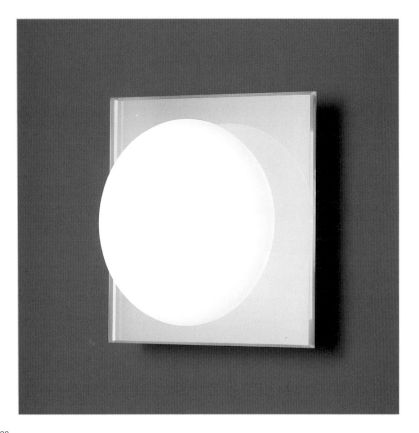

⊙⊙ **Giò** Wall and ceiling lamps with central frosted glass shade. The square back plate is available in orange, white, blue, frosted, lemon yellow, or apple green glass, or mirror, wengé, or brushed nickel. *Michele Sbrogiò*

⊙● **Giò** Hanging lamp with frosted white glass shade. The frame is in glass and available in orange, white, blue, frosted, lemon yellow, black, red, apple green, or mirrored glass, or in stainless steel. The support is metal lacquered silver. *Michele Sbrogiò*

⊙⊙ **Quadra** Wall and ceiling lamps with central frosted glass shade. The back plate is available in amber, frosted, fuschia, or diamond glass. The body is metal lacquered silver. *Michele Sbrogiò*

**Popone** Hanging lamp with dichroic wide-beam projector bulb. The bulb can be directed upwards or downwards. The body is transparent hand-blown borosilicate glass. *Album*

**Loop** Table lamp with stainless steel or varnished nickel body. The on/off switch is operated by rotating the upper piece of the body. *Voon Wong*

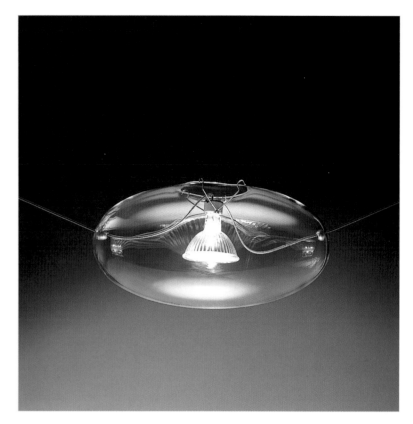

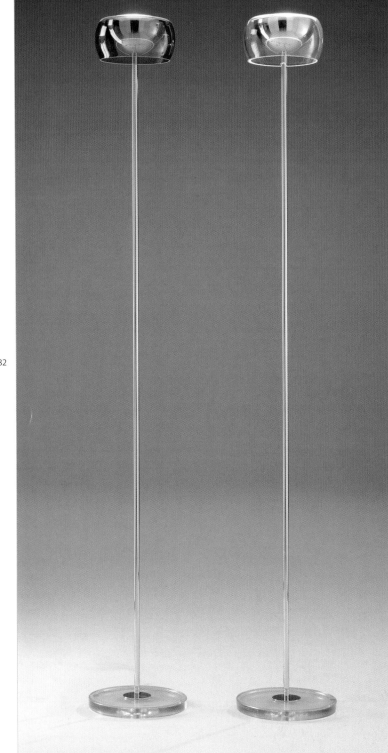

**Aura Terra** Standing lamp with brilliant chromed metal body and glass base. The shade is transparent blown glass available in orange or green. *Mauro Marzollo*

**Omega** Wall lamp with transparent acrylic glass shade. The shade is also available in blue, yellow, and red. *Arter+Citton*

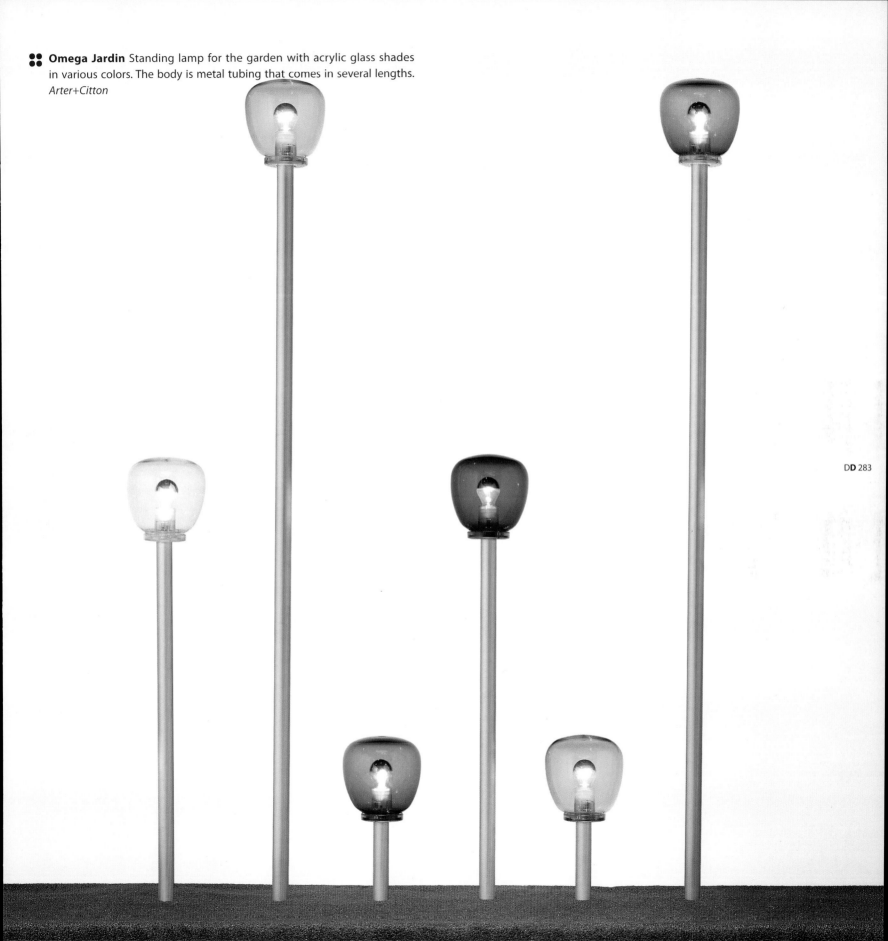

**Omega Jardin** Standing lamp for the garden with acrylic glass shades in various colors. The body is metal tubing that comes in several lengths.
*Arter+Citton*

DD 283

⠠ **Oriente** Series of ceiling, table, wall, and floor lamps with silvered metal body. The blown glass shades are available in aquamarine, amber, crystal, and white. *Crepax & Zanon*

**Guardia** Series of standing and table lamps with wooden bodies and varnished gold or silver bases. The shade is silk. *Adolfo Fabbio*

**Royal Oversize F** Floor and ceiling lamps with stainless steel bodies and pleated fabric shades. *David Abad*

 **Optica** Wall and floor lamps with polished aluminum bodies. The cylindrical shades are transparent acrylic plastic lined with optical lighting film. *Zed*

**Zenith** Ceiling lamp with chromed steel body. The shade around the halogen bulb is metal. *Di Vetro*

**Onion** Hanging lamp with transparent glass shade and chromed metal body. *Mario Marenco*

**Rx** Table lamp with chromed steel. The spiral-shaped shade is opaque hand-molded glass. *Di Vetro*

DD 289

**P-Rex** Hanging lamp with matte white glass shades. *Massimo Lunardon*

**Rotondo** Candle-shaped lamp made of semitransparent glass available in different colors. It has a rechargeable battery. *Traxon*

**Bild Candle** Candle-shaped lamp with metal body and silicone and semitransparent glass shade. It has a rechargeable battery. *Traxon*

**Cooler** Lamp shaped like an ice bucket. The body is plastic and semitransparent glass, available in several colors. The base is aluminum. It has a rechargeable battery. *Traxon*

**KPMG** Colored light system intended for the decoration of staircases and other large areas. *Ingo Maurer*

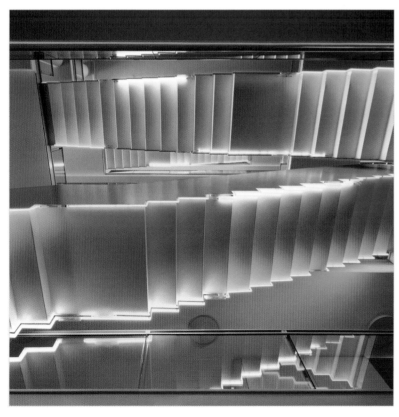

**Luster** Hanging lamp made of printed glass panel with red or black LEDs embedded. *Ingo Maurer*

**Shikakku** Table lamp with metal body lacquered black outside and red inside. *Hiroshi Tsunoda*

DD 293

**Sixties** Series of floor and ceiling lamps with metal bodies lacquered in black or white. *Enric Gregorio*

**Cuore Aperto** Sculptural heart-shaped lamp, surrounded by the designer's signature birds. *Ingo Maurer*

 **Hearts Attack** Hanging lamp made up of forty-eight adjustable synthetic mirror hearts and one twelve-volt bulb. *Ingo Maurer*

**One from the Heart** Table lamp with metal body, heart-shaped plastic shade, and heart-shaped mirror reflector. *Ingo Maurer*

**Spyra** Standing lamp with spiral-shaped shade made of matte white Murano glass. *Crepax & Zanon*

**Aba** Table lamp with neutral or colored opalescent resin shade. The body is hand-turned terracotta with natural, opaque white, or metal finishes. *Album*

:: **Accento** Table lamp with glass body and shade. The switch is built into the cable, which leads straight up the tube to the dichroic halogen bulb. *Album*

:: **Danzatrici** Standing lamp with a curved steel stem and handmade frosted glass shade. *Album*

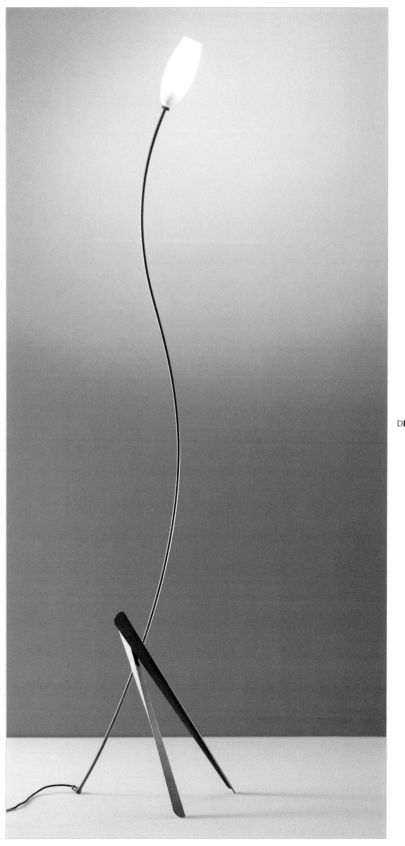

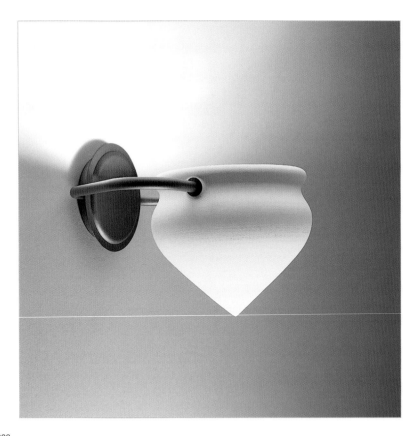
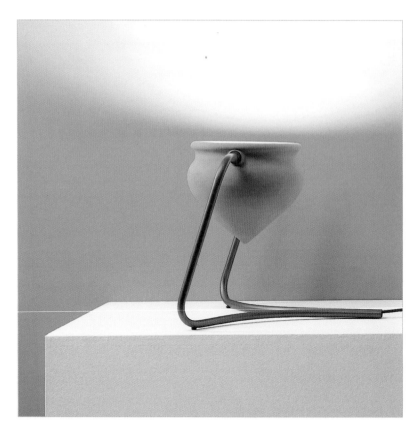

⠿ **Dòlio** Series of lamps with luminous bodies on metal supports. The terracotta shade is handmade and available in several finishes. *Album*

**Fili** Series of hanging lamps available with transparent glass stems in various shapes to direct light in different directions. *Album*

⣿ **Viva** Series of lamps in four sizes available with bodies in metal, glass, or a variety of varnishes. The shade is also available in several different shapes. *Heinz Klein and Georg Leidig*

⣿ **Bella** Series of lamps in different sizes with bodies available in any matte or high-gloss colored varnish. The shade is silk. *Fitz Licht*

DD 301

**Falò** Table lamp with terracotta body that accommodates a large number of candle bulbs. *Album*

**Fili d'Angelo** Series of hanging lamps available with transparent borosilicate or painted Murano glass stems in various shapes to direct light in different directions. *Album*

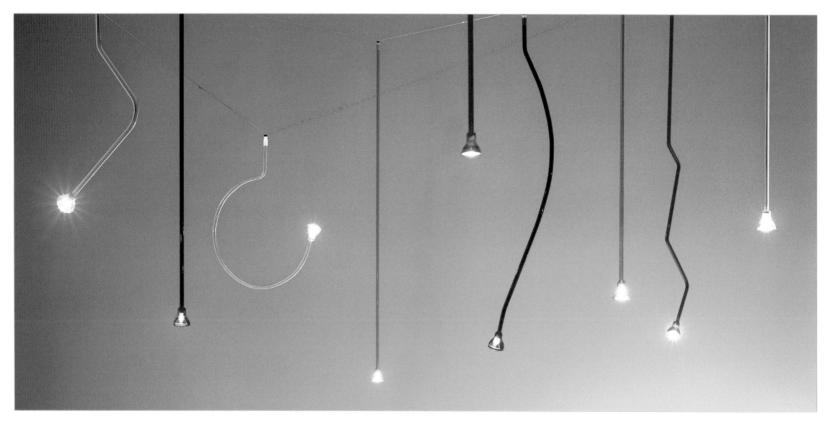

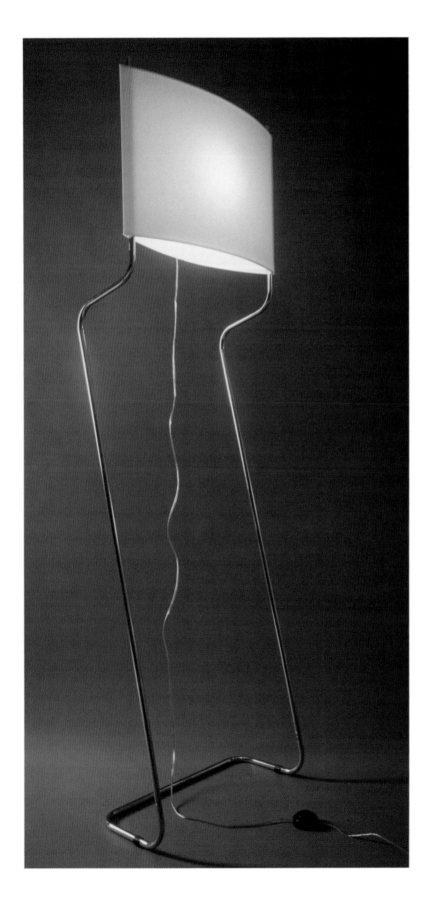

**Oog** Standing lamp with metallic base and cretonne shade. The fabric of the shade can be white or printed cotton. *Marc Th. Van der Voorn*

**Relax** Adjustable or fixed wall lamp with white or gray varnished metal body and shade in eggshell white acrylic glass. *Defne Koz*

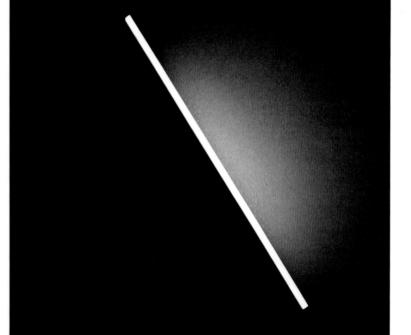

**Alata** Directional and adjustable standing lamp with steel body varnished with silver epoxy powder. The steel laminate shade has a halogen bulb. *Zed*

**El.E.Dee** Table lamp with stainless steel and metal body. The LED lights are embedded in a circuit board that is mounted with a ball-and-socket joint to allow easy adjustment. *Ingo Maurer*

**Gilda** Standing lamp on anodized aluminum extendible body in natural or polished finish. The large shade is synthetic ivory or white parchment, and the lamp is fitted with a dimmer. *Enrico Franzolini*

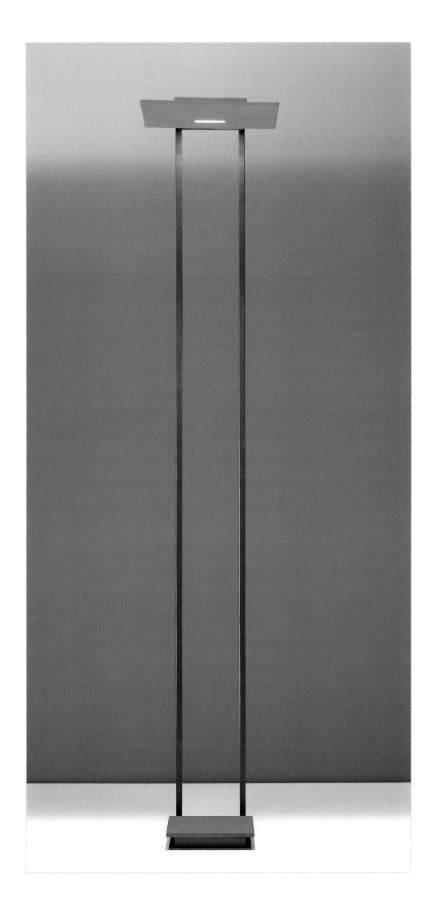

**Pianella** Series of wall and floor lamps with terracotta shades available in natural, matte white, or metal finishes. A small cut in the bottom of the shade allows light to escape. The body is metal. *Album*

**Viva Casa** The smallest in a range of lamps available with bodies in metal, glass, or a variety of varnishes. The shade is also available in several different shapes. *Heinz Klein and Georg Leidig*

 **Luna** Table lamp made of different materials, all colored the same gold tint. The metal sphere supporting the shade can be tilted. *Fitz Licht*

 **Boveda** Table lamp with refined metal body and a silk shade available in several colors. There is an extra bulb mounted between the metal legs. *Fitz Licht*

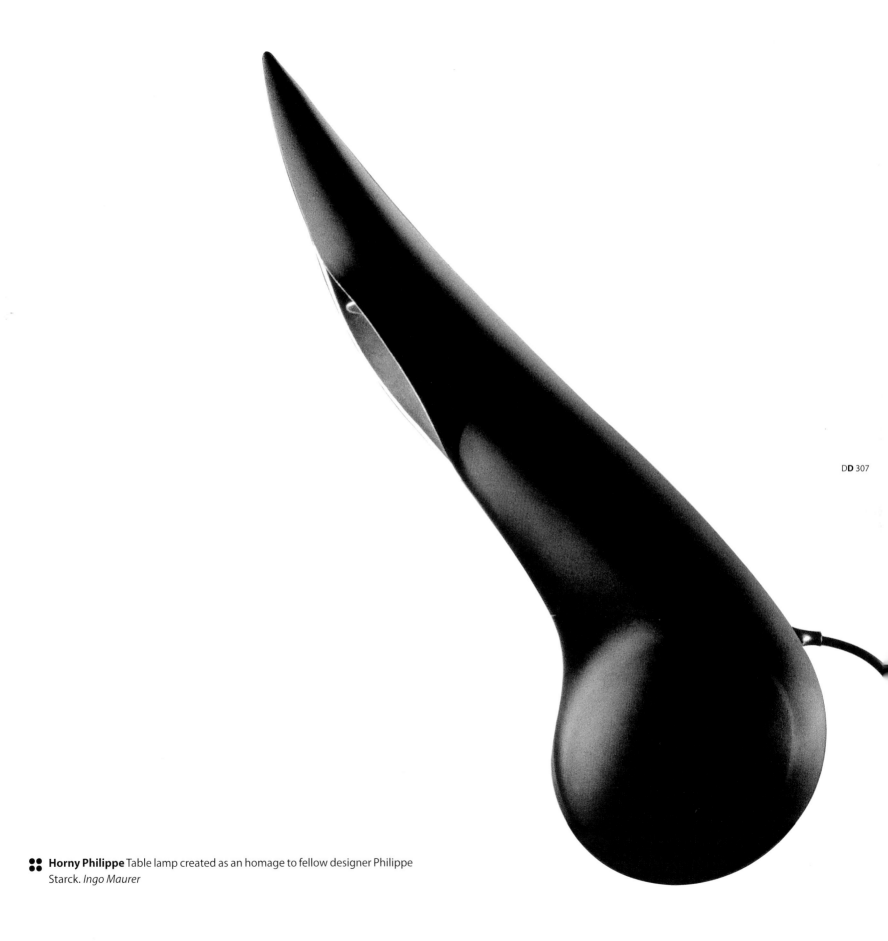

DD 307

⣿ **Horny Philippe** Table lamp created as an homage to fellow designer Philippe Starck. *Ingo Maurer*

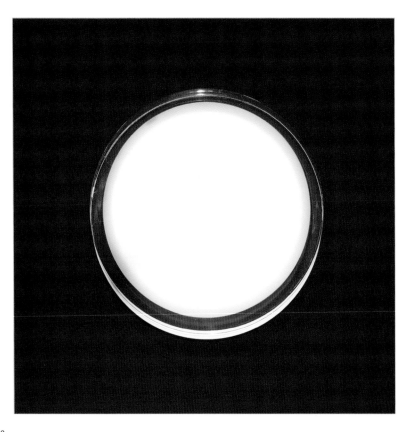

●● **Lunaplena** Wall or hanging lamp with white varnished metal body and matte white polymethacrylate shade. *Roberto Righetti*

●● **Zibor Color** Wall lamp with metallic body. The shade is acrylic glass, and the piece can be mounted on any surface or used as a built-in light. *Miguel Angel Ciganda*

**Zorro** Standing or wall lamp with low-tension dichroic projector bulbs, each of which can be adjusted separately. The body is steel and can accommodate up to four bulbs. *Album*

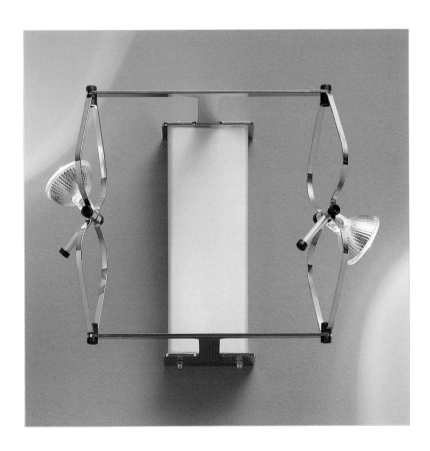

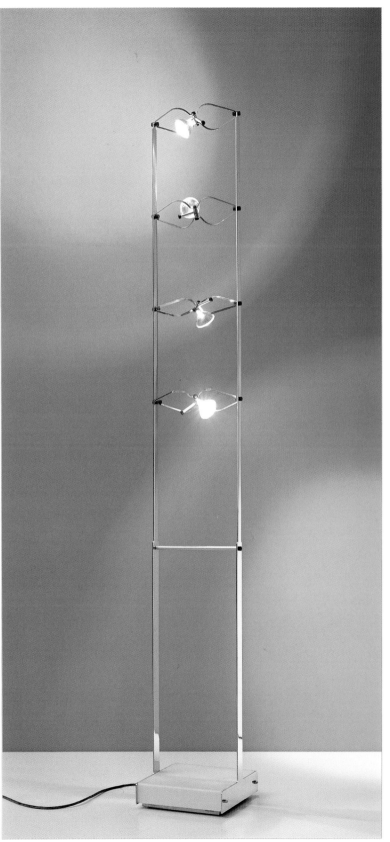

DD 309

**Bella** Standing or ceiling lamp with metallic nickel or black body. The shade is available in opaque white or transparent blown glass. *Harry & Camila*

**Carlotta** Hanging lamp with gray varnished metal body. The shade is blown glass with details in transparent, amber, red, or green glass. *Giusto Toso*

**A Tomic** Hanging lamp available in two sizes. The body is chromed metal, and the shade is matte white blown glass. *Paolo Zani*

**Zibor S** A hanging lamp with metal body and acrylic glass shade. *Miguel Angel Ciganda*

DD 311

**Ote** Symmetrical table lamp with folded sheet metal shade and body finished in iron black or aluminum on the outside and colored on the inside. *Antoni Arola*

DD 312

●● **Prototipo** Series of table, clamp, and floor lamps with metal base. The body
○○ and shade are made of aluminum, stainless steel, and silicone. *Ingo Maurer,
Bernhard Dessecker*

●● **One by One** Table lamp with shade made from Nomex, a recyclable, tear-
●○ proof fabric created by DuPont. The layers of parchment-like Nomex diffuse
the light from the central bulb. *Steve Lechot*

●● **Candle Lamp** Metal lamps intended to house candles. The frame is painted
○○ black, and the shade is plastic. *Conmoto*

●● **Lampampe** Table lamp with metal body completely covered in Japanese paper. *Ingo Maurer*

●● **Johnny B. Good** Hanging lamp made of glass, Teflon, and plastic, with attached cable. *Ingo Maurer, Bernhard Dessecker*

**Electra** Hanging lamp with elongated aluminum shade available in silver, blue, or orange. Each piece uses six halogen bulbs. *Christoph Steinemann*

**Canned** Table or ceiling lamp with shade made from Campbell's soup can. The body is aluminum, stainless steel, and plastic. *Christoph Matthias, Hagen Sczech*

**Bacco 1 2 3** Bottle-shaped lamps in various sizes. The frosted Murano glass shades are available in amber, yellow, and frosted green, and the "corks" are brilliant sky blue. The base is metal varnished dark gray. *Guido Rosati*

**Ghost** Table lamps with metal base lacquered with dark gray epoxy powder. The frosted glass shades have transparent "eyes" cut out in white. *Carlo Nason*

**Class 40/60** Hanging metallic gray lamp sets in two sizes. These lights can be mounted on a track in sets of two to five lamps. *Ufficio Stile I Tre*

**Abyss** Hanging lamp with transparent and frosted blown glass shade. The support is chromed metal, and the light can be installed with a track or a plain ceiling fixture. *Ufficio Stile Aureliano Toso*

# Designer Directory

## A

Aanuit www.aanuit.nl
Acerbis www.acerbisinternational.com
Afroditi Krassa www.afroditi.com
Album www.album.it
Alexander Lervik www.alexanderlervik.com
Álvaro Siza Vieira www.bdbarcelona.com
Annell www.annell.se
Antoni Arola www.bdbarcelona.com
Antoni de Moragas www.bdbarcelona.com
Artifort www.artifort.com
Azcue www.azcue.com
Azioni www.azioniprivilegiate.it

## B

B-lux www.grupobelux.com, www.ansorg.com
Bellato www.palluccobellato.it
Biplax www.biplax.com
Black & Blum www.black-blum.com
Brühl www.bruehl.com
Büro für Form www.buerofuerform.de
Buro Vormkrijgers www.burovormkrijgers.nl

## C

Cantori www.cantori.it
Cattellan Italia www.cattelanitalia.com
Chris Slutter www.chrisslutter.nl
Conmoto www.conmoto.com
Cor www.cor.de

## D

Dab www.dab.es
Demacker design www.demacker-design.de
Design Afairs www.designafairs.com
Diplomat www.diplomat.org.uk

## E

Elmar Flototto www.elmarfloetotto.de
Elmar Thome www.bdbarcelona.com
Enric Soria www.bdbarcelona.com

## F

Firme Di Vetro www.firmedivetro.com
Fitz Licht www.fitz-licht.de
Fly Line www.flyline.it
Fontana arte www.fontanaarte.it
Foscarini www.foscarini.com
Fritz Hansen www.fritzhansen.com
Fuseproject www.fuseproject.com
Fynn www.shaunfynn.com

## G

Gandia Blasco www.gandiablasco.com
Goods www.goods.nl

## H

Horm www.horm.it

## I

Iguzzini www.iguzzini.com
Industris 191 www.industris191.de
Ingo Maurer www.ingo-maurer.com
Intoto www.intotonyc.com
Iosa Ghini www.iosaghini.it
IP 44 www.ip44.de

## J

John Greg Ball www.johngregball.com
Jonathan Daifuku www.daifukudesigns.com
Jordi Garcés www.bdbarcelona.com

**K**

Kidino www.kidino.com
Komplot www.komplot.dk
Kundalini www.palluccobellato.it

**L**

Lago www.lago.it
Leds C-4 www.leds-c4.com
Lindner www.lindnerimnorden.com
Lookiluz www.lookiluz.com

**M**

Matali Crasset www.matalicrasset.com
Matthew Hilton www.bdbarcelona.com
Miguel Milá www.bdbarcelona.com
MNO design www.mnodesign.nl
Molteni www.molteni.it
Montis www.montis.nl
Moobel www.moobel.ch
Moroso www.moroso.it

**O**

OeO www.oeostudio.com
Offecct www.offecct.se
Orizzonti www.orizzonti-srl.com
Oscar Tusquets www.tusquets.com

**P**

Pallucco www.palluccobellato.it
Pepe Cortés www.bdbarcelona.com
Perobell www.perobell.com
PH Collection www.ph-collection.com
Porro www.porro.com

**Q**

Quasar www.quasar.nl

**R**

Rafemar www.rafemar.com
Roberto Monte www.m2design.it

**S**

Satyendra Pakhalé www.satyendra-pakhale.com
Scabetti www.scabetti.co.uk
Stokke Tok www.stokke.com

**T**

Tam-Tam www.tamtam-branex.com
Theo Williams www.theowilliams.com
Thonet www.thonet.de
Traxon www.traxongroup.com

**V**

Valvomo www.valvomo.com
Victoria www.fabioluciani.it

**W**

Walter Knoll www.walterknoll.de
Wittmann www.wittmann.at
WK Wohnen www.wkwohnen.de

**X**

Xavier Lust www.xavierlust.com

**Z**

Zeitraum www.zeitraum-moebel.de

Art Director, original English-language edition Lorena Paula Damonte
Editor, original English-language edition Silvana Díaz
Packager, original English-language edition Linea Editorial

Project Manager, North American edition Aiah R. Wieder
Designer, North American edition Shawn Dahl
Production Manager, North American edition Anet Sirna-Bruder

Library of Congress Cataloging-in-Publication Data
Asensio, Oscar.
   [DesignDesign. English]
   DesignDesign : furniture & lights / by Oscar Asensio.
      p. cm. — (DesignDesign)
   ISBN-13: 978-0-8109-9294-8 (hardcover)
   ISBN-10: 0-8109-9294-9
   1. Furniture design—History—21st century.  2. Lighting—History—21st century.
   I. Title. II. Title: Design design : furniture and lights.
   NK2399.2.A8413 2007
   749.09′05--dc22
                              2006034261

Printed and bound in China
10 9 8 7 6 5 4 3 2 1

HNA
harry n. abrams, inc.
a subsidiary of La Martinière Groupe

115 West 18th Street
New York, NY 10011
www.hnabooks.com